Mockito for Spring

Learn all you need to know about the Spring Framework
and how to unit test your projects with Mockito

Sujoy Acharya

open source*
community experience distilled

PUBLISHING

BIRMINGHAM - MUMBAI

Mockito for Spring

First published: February 2015

Production reference: 1200215

Published by Packt Publishing Ltd.
Livery Place
35 Livery Street
Birmingham B3 2PB, UK.

ISBN 978-1-78398-378-0

www.packtpub.com

Credits

Author
Sujoy Acharya

Reviewers
Carlo Micieli

Gualtiero Testa

Commissioning Editor
Amarabha Banerjee

Acquisition Editor
Llewellyn Rozario

Content Development Editor
Parita Khedekar

Technical Editors
Manal Pednekar

Chinmay S. Puranik

Copy Editors
Dipti Kapadia

Deepa Nambiar

Vikrant Phadke

Project Coordinator
Milton Dsouza

Proofreaders
Martin Diver

Maria Gould

Paul Hindle

Indexer
Monica Ajmera Mehta

Production Coordinator
Aparna Bhagat

Cover Work
Aparna Bhagat

About the Author

Sujoy Acharya works as a software architect with Siemens Technology and Services Pvt. Ltd. (STS). He grew up in a joint family and pursued his graduation in the fields of computer science and engineering. His hobbies are watching movies and sitcoms, playing outdoor sports, and reading books.

Sujoy likes to research upcoming technologies. His major contributions are in the fields of Java, J2EE, SOA, Ajax, GWT, and the Spring Framework.

He has authored three books for Packt Publishing, namely *Test-Driven Development with Mockito*, *Mastering Unit Testing using Mockito and JUnit*, and *Mockito Essentials*.

He designs and develops healthcare software products. He has over 11 years of experience in the industry and has architected and implemented large-scale enterprise solutions.

I'd especially like to thank my wife, Sunanda, firstly for pushing me to man up and finish the book, and additionally, for her patience and endless support in the many hours spent on reviewing my draft and providing valuable inputs.

I would also like to thank my mother and late father for their support, blessings, and encouragement.

To my 23-month-old kid, Abhigyan, I am sorry I couldn't be around as much as we all wanted and for the many times I had to get you away from the laptop. I love you very much.

About the Reviewers

Carlo Micieli has been a software developer since 2001, developing applications for computer-aided manufacturing with C#.

His main area of interest is application life cycle management, with a strong focus on topics such as software design and testing.

He is a programming languages enthusiast, and he's currently trying to learn Scala and Haskell. He shares his experiments on GitHub (`http://github.com/CarloMicieli`).

Gualtiero Testa is a software analyst, architect, and developer involved in Java enterprise-level web applications, mainly in the domains of banking, health, and government agencies. He lives in Pavia, Italy.

His main interests are test-driven development (TDD), testing tools and methodologies, and everything related to code quality.

You can reach him through his blog at `http://www.gualtierotesta.it/`.

I would like to thank my wife, Alessandra, and my daughters, Giulia and Francesca, because they are the source of my happiness.

www.PacktPub.com

Support files, eBooks, discount offers, and more

For support files and downloads related to your book, please visit www.PacktPub.com.

Did you know that Packt offers eBook versions of every book published, with PDF and ePub files available? You can upgrade to the eBook version at www.PacktPub.com and as a print book customer, you are entitled to a discount on the eBook copy. Get in touch with us at service@packtpub.com for more details.

At www.PacktPub.com, you can also read a collection of free technical articles, sign up for a range of free newsletters, and receive exclusive discounts and offers on Packt books and eBooks.

https://www2.packtpub.com/books/subscription/packtlib

Do you need instant solutions to your IT questions? PacktLib is Packt's online digital book library. Here, you can search, access, and read Packt's entire library of books.

Why subscribe?

- Fully searchable across every book published by Packt
- Copy and paste, print, and bookmark content
- On demand and accessible via a web browser

Free access for Packt account holders

If you have an account with Packt at www.PacktPub.com, you can use this to access PacktLib today and view nine entirely free books. Simply use your login credentials for immediate access.

Table of Contents

Preface

When I was writing the first draft of this book, I was eager to compare the manuscript with other books on the Spring Framework. Here are the features that distinguish this book from others:

- This book is not only about the Spring Framework. It also describes the basics of Spring, Spring's test module, Spring's integration testing, JUnit testing, how to mock Spring beans with Mockito, and advanced Spring 4.1 features. I couldn't find any books that cover these topics.
- This book explains JUnit testing and mocking in the context of Spring.
- The book covers Spring's test module and Spring integration testing in detail. These are the most difficult parts in the Spring testing world.

I have taken a hands-on approach here by combining theories with examples to explain the topics.

What this book covers

Chapter 1, Getting Familiar with the Spring Framework, covers the basics of Spring, Spring projects, and especially the Spring Framework. It explores the Spring container, the life cycle of beans, dependency injection, AOP, Spring MVC, and Spring transaction management.

Chapter 2, Working with JUnit and Mockito, covers both basic and advanced JUnit usages. It covers annotation-based JUnit testing, assertion, the `@RunWith` annotation, exception handling, and the Eclipse setup to run JUnit tests, matchers, and `assertThat`, as well as the custom `lessThanOrEqual()` matcher. The *Working with Mockito* section explores the Mockito framework and provides technical examples to demonstrate the capability of Mockito.

Chapter 3, Working with Spring Tests, illustrates every aspect of unit testing your Spring applications. It starts with `TestContext` and explores the JUnit 4 enabled `SpringJUnit4ClassRunner`. Then, it explores Spring profiles that can be used to work with the different sets of configuration files as well as the Spring environment and how to mock the environment with `MockEnvironment` and `MockPropertySource`. We use the `ReflectionTestUtils` method to access the private fields of the Spring beans. The chapter provides usage examples of Spring annotations for testing, unit tests the MVC application with `MockHttpServletRequest, MockHttpSession,` and `ModelAndViewAssert,` and mocks the servlet container with `MockMvc` to handle actual requests and responses, as they will be at runtime. You will also perform real Spring integration and transaction management with annotations such as `@Transactional,` `@TransactionConfiguration,` and `@Rollback`.

Chapter 4, Resolving Out-of-container Dependencies with Mockito, deals with unit testing the service layer in isolation from the data access layer with Mockito, unit testing the Spring data access layer with Mockito, and unit testing the Spring presentation layer (MVC) with Mockito.

Chapter 5, Time Travelling with Spring, starts by covering the features of the new major Spring release 4.0, such as Java 8 support and so on. Then, we pick the four Spring 4 topics and explore them one by one. The *Working with asynchronous tasks* section showcases the execution of long running methods asynchronously and provides examples to handle asynchronous processing. The *Exploring @RestController* section eases RESTful web service development with the advent of the `@RestController` annotation. The *Learning AsyncRestTemplate* section explains the RESTful client code to invoke RESTful web services asynchronously. Caching is inevitable for high performant, scalable web applications. This section explains EhCache and Spring integration to achieve a high availability caching solution.

What you need for this book

You will need the following software installed before you run the examples:

- Java 7 or higher: JDK 1.7 or higher can be downloaded from `http://www.oracle.com/technetwork/java/javase/downloads/index.html`.
- Eclipse editor: The latest version of Eclipse is Luna (4.4.1), which can be downloaded from `http://www.eclipse.org/downloads/`.
- Mockito: This is required for the creation and verification of mock objects and for stubbing. Mockito can be downloaded from `https://code.google.com/p/mockito/downloads/list`.
- Spring modules: These are used for coding and testing. Spring JARs can be downloaded from `http://maven.springframework.org/release/org/springframework/spring/`.

Who this book is for

This book is for advanced and novice-level software testers/developers using the Spring Framework, Mockito, and JUnit. You should have a reasonable amount of knowledge and understanding of unit testing elements and applications.

It is ideal for developers who have some experience in Java application development and the Spring Framework as well as some basic knowledge of JUnit testing. However, it also covers the basic fundamentals of JUnit testing, the Spring Framework, and the Mockito framework to get you acquainted with these concepts before you use them.

Conventions

In this book, you will find a number of styles of text that distinguish between different kinds of information. Here are some examples of these styles, and an explanation of their meaning.

Code words in text, database table names, folder names, filenames, file extensions, pathnames, dummy URLs, user input, and Twitter handles are shown as follows: "The messaging module comes with key abstractions from the Spring Integration project such as `Message`, `MessageChannel`, and `MessageHandler` to serve as a foundation for messaging-based applications."

A block of code is set as follows:

```
@Test
public void currencyRoundsOff() throws Exception {
  assertNotNull(CurrencyFormatter.format(100.999));
  assertTrue(CurrencyFormatter.format(100.999).
    contains("$"));
  assertEquals("$101.00", CurrencyFormatter.format(100.999));
}
```

When we wish to draw your attention to a particular part of a code block, the relevant lines or items are set in bold:

```
public class LocaleTest {
  private Locale defaultLocale;
  @Before
  public void setUp() {
    defaultLocale = Locale.getDefault();
    Locale.setDefault(Locale.GERMANY);
  }
```

```
@After
public void restore() {
  Locale.setDefault(defaultLocale);
}
@Test
public void currencyRoundsOff() throws Exception {
  assertEquals("$101.00", CurrencyFormatter.format(100.999));
}
}
```

New terms and **important words** are shown in bold. Words that you see on the screen, in menus or dialog boxes for example, appear in the text like this: "Right-click on the project; a pop-up menu will appear. Expand the **Build Path** menu and click on the **Configure Build Path** menu item."

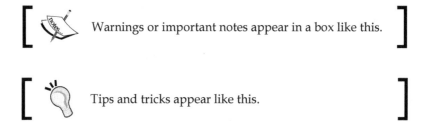

Warnings or important notes appear in a box like this.

Tips and tricks appear like this.

Reader feedback

Feedback from our readers is always welcome. Let us know what you think about this book—what you liked or may have disliked. Reader feedback is important for us to develop titles that you really get the most out of.

To send us general feedback, simply send an e-mail to feedback@packtpub.com, and mention the book title via the subject of your message.

If there is a topic that you have expertise in and you are interested in either writing or contributing to a book, see our author guide on www.packtpub.com/authors.

Customer support

Now that you are the proud owner of a Packt book, we have a number of things to help you to get the most from your purchase.

Downloading the example code

You can download the example code files for all Packt books you have purchased from your account at http://www.packtpub.com. If you purchased this book elsewhere, you can visit http://www.packtpub.com/support and register to have the files e-mailed directly to you.

Errata

Although we have taken every care to ensure the accuracy of our content, mistakes do happen. If you find a mistake in one of our books—maybe a mistake in the text or the code—we would be grateful if you would report this to us. By doing so, you can save other readers from frustration and help us improve subsequent versions of this book. If you find any errata, please report them by visiting http://www.packtpub.com/submit-errata, selecting your book, clicking on the **errata submission form** link, and entering the details of your errata. Once your errata are verified, your submission will be accepted and the errata will be uploaded on our website, or added to any list of existing errata, under the Errata section of that title. Any existing errata can be viewed by selecting your title from http://www.packtpub.com/support.

Piracy

Piracy of copyright material on the Internet is an ongoing problem across all media. At Packt, we take the protection of our copyright and licenses very seriously. If you come across any illegal copies of our works, in any form, on the Internet, please provide us with the location address or website name immediately so that we can pursue a remedy.

Please contact us at copyright@packtpub.com with a link to the suspected pirated material.

We appreciate your help in protecting our authors, and our ability to bring you valuable content.

Questions

You can contact us at questions@packtpub.com if you are having a problem with any aspect of the book, and we will do our best to address it.

1
Getting Familiar with the Spring Framework

Spring is a popular enterprise application development framework. This chapter covers the following topics:

- Spring Framework fundamentals
- Spring projects
- The Spring architecture and modules
- **Inversion of control (IoC)** and **dependency injection (DI)**
- Setting up a Spring development environment, a Hello World program, and autowiring
- **Aspect-oriented Programming (AOP)**
- Spring JDBC
- Transaction management
- Spring MVC

Getting started with Spring

Spring is an open source enterprise application development framework for Java. It was first written by Rod Johnson and released under the Apache 2.0 license in June 2003.

Spring Framework provides comprehensive infrastructure support for developing Java applications. Spring handles the infrastructure for us and allows us to focus on our application logic. Spring enables us to build applications from **Plain Old Java Objects (POJOs)** and apply enterprise services non-invasively to POJOs.

The following are examples of POJO-based application development:

- A Java method can handle an HTTP POST/GET request; you don't have to write a servlet or work with servlet APIs

- A Java method can act as a RESTful web service without dealing with web service APIs

- A Java method can execute a database transaction without dealing with transaction APIs

- A local Java method can participate in a **remote procedure call** (**RPC**) without having to deal with remote APIs

- A Java method can consume or handle messages without having to deal with JMS APIs

- A Java method can work as a management extension without dealing with JMX APIs

In a nutshell, Spring can be described as follows:

- An open source application framework
- One of the available enterprise application frameworks and a lightweight solution for enterprise applications
- Non-invasive (POJO-based)
- Modular
- Extensible for other frameworks
- The de facto standard of Java enterprise applications

The following are advantages of Spring:

- Lightweight and minimally invasive development with POJOs
- Loose coupling through dependency injection and interface-orientation
- Declarative programming through aspects and common conventions
- Boilerplate code reduction through aspects and templates

Spring projects provide infrastructure for building security configuration, web applications, big data, LDAP, and so on. Spring Framework is one of the Spring projects.

There are various Spring projects that can be used. In this book, we'll be using Spring 4.

The following are the icons of some Spring projects:

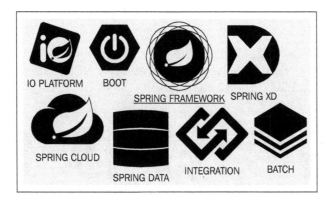

The following are all Spring projects as of September 2014:

- **The Spring IO platform**: Spring IO brings together the core Spring APIs into a cohesive and versioned foundational platform for modern applications. Spring IO is comprised of the Spring IO Foundation and Spring IO Execution layers.

- **Spring Boot**: This helps in creating production-grade Spring applications that can be run any time with the minimal Spring configuration. It follows the convention-over-configuration approach.

- **Spring Framework**: This is an open source framework for Java enterprise applications. It provides an inversion of control container for Java beans. The framework offers a number of templates for the developers; the templates hide the infrastructure code and allow us to concentrate on the business logic.

- **Spring XD**: This is a unified, distributed, and extensible system for data ingestion, real-time analytics, batch processing, and data export. The goal of the project is to simplify the development of big data applications.

- **Spring Cloud**: Spring Cloud builds on Spring Boot by providing a bunch of libraries that enhance the behavior of an application when added to the classpath. You can take advantage of the basic default behavior to get started really quickly, and then when you need to, you can configure or extend it to create a custom solution.

- **Spring Data**: This simplifies data access, offers APIs to work with the relational databases, NoSQL or non-relational databases, big data or the map-reduce algorithm, and so on.

- **Spring Integration**: This follows **Enterprise Integration Patterns (EIP)** to enable us lightweight, POJO-based messaging for Spring applications to integrate with external systems.

- **Spring Batch**: This is a lightweight, comprehensive batch framework designed to enable the development of robust batch applications vital for the daily operations of enterprise systems.

  The following image displays the icons of the following spring projects: security, HATEOAS, social, AMQP, web services, Mobile, Android, web flow, Spring LDAP and Grails

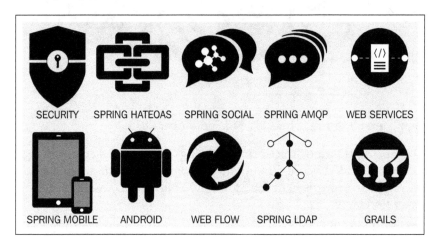

- **Spring Security**: This is a powerful and highly customizable authentication and access-control framework. It is the de facto standard for securing Spring-based applications.

- **Spring HATEOAS**: This allows you to create REST representations that follow the HATEOAS principle from your Spring-based applications.

- **Spring Social**: Connect your Spring application with **Software as a Service (SaaS)** API providers such as Facebook, Twitter, and LinkedIn.

- **Spring AMQP**: The **Advanced Message Queuing Protocol (AMQP)** is an open standard for messaging. Spring AMQP offers solutions for AMQP-based messaging, for example, it can be used with the AMQP broker RabbitMQ.

- **Spring Mobile**: This is an extension to Spring MVC that aims to simplify the development of mobile web applications.

- **Spring for Android**: This is an extension of Spring Framework that aims to simplify the development of native Android applications.

- **Spring Web Flow**: This provides the infrastructure to build process workflows for web-based Spring applications, such as page navigation, navigation triggers, application state, and services to invoke. This is stateful and can be a short-lived process flow or long-running flow.

- **Spring Web Services**: This aims to facilitate contract-first SOAP service development, and this allows the creation of flexible web services using one of the many ways to manipulate XML payloads.

- **Spring LDAP**: This makes it easier to build Spring-based applications that use the **Lightweight Directory Access Protocol (LDAP)**.

Exploring the Spring architecture

Spring Framework is modular, and its features are organized into different modules. This section talks about core Spring modules. The following are the Spring 4 modules:

The core container

The core container holds the backbone of Spring Framework. The following are the submodules in the core container:

- **Core and Beans**: These provide the fundamental parts of the framework, including IoC and dependency injection features

- **Context**: This is a means to access objects in a framework-style manner that is similar to the JNDI registry

- **Expression Language**: This is also known as SpEL; it is an expression language used to query and modify an object graph and evaluate mathematical expressions

The AOP module

AOP is an aspect-oriented programming implementation of Spring. It decouples the business logic from the cross-cutting infrastructure code, such as logging and security.

The instrumentation module

The instrumentation module provides class instrumentation support for the Spring application. Instrumentation exposes container resources through MBean and helps in JMX management.

The messaging module

The messaging module comes with key abstractions from the Spring Integration project such as `Message`, `MessageChannel`, and `MessageHandler` to serve as a foundation for messaging-based applications.

The data access module

The following are the submodules in the data access module:

- **JDBC**: This provides a JDBC abstraction layer
- **ORM**: This provides integration layers for popular object-relational mapping APIs, including JPA, JDO, Hibernate, and iBATIS
- **OXM**: This provides an abstraction layer that supports object/XML mapping implementations for `JAXB`, `Castor`, `XMLBeans`, `JiBX`, and `Xstream`
- **JMS**: This contains features to produce and consume messages
- **Transactions**: This supports programmatic and declarative transaction management

The web layer

The web layer consists of the web, webmvc/servlet, WebSocket, and webmvc-portlet modules:

- **Web**: This module provides basic web-oriented integration features such as multipart file upload functionality and initialization of the IoC container using servlet listeners and web-oriented application context. It also contains the web-related parts of Spring's remoting support.
- **Webmvc**: This module (also known as the web-servlet module) contains Spring's model-view-controller implementation for web applications. Spring's MVC framework provides a clean separation between the domain model code and web forms and integrates with all the other features of Spring Framework.
- **Portlet**: This module (also known as the web-portlet module) provides the MVC implementation to be used in a portlet environment and mirrors the functionality of the webmvc module.
- **WebSocket**: This module provides APIs for two-way communication between client and server. It is extremely useful when the client and server need to exchange events at high frequency and low latency. Prime candidates include applications in finance, games, collaboration, and so on.

The test module

The test module supports the unit testing and integration testing of Spring components with JUnit or TestNG.

The following figure represents the Spring 4 modules:

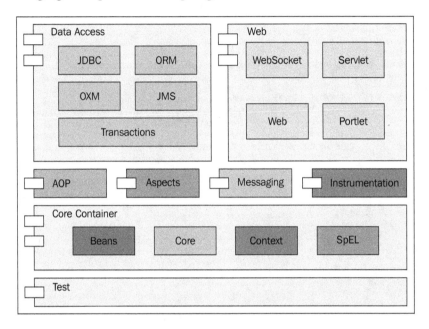

Learning the Inversion of Control

Inversion of Control (IoC) and **dependency injection (DI)** are used interchangeably. IoC is achieved through DI. DI is the process of providing dependencies and IoC is the end result of DI. Spring's IoC container enforces the DI pattern for your components, and this leaves them loosely coupled and allows you to code to abstractions.

Dependency injection is a style of object configuration in which an object's fields and collaborators are set by an external entity. In other words, objects are configured by an external entity. Dependency injection is an alternative to having the object configure itself. This might sound a bit vague, so let's look at a simple example.

After visiting the Packt Publishing website, you can search books by the author's name or different criteria. We'll look at the service that lists books by author.

The following interface defines book retrieval:

```
public interface BookService {
  List<Book> findAll();
}
```

The following class lists books by author names:

```
public class BookLister {

  private BookService bookFinder = new BookServiceImpl();

  public List<Book> findByAuthor(String author){
    List<Book> books = new ArrayList<>();

    for(Book aBook:bookFinder.findAll()){
      for(String anAuthor:aBook.getAuthors()){
        if(anAuthor.equals(author)){
          books.add(aBook);
          break;
        }
      }
    }

    return books;
  }

}
```

The `BookLister` class needs a `BookService` implementation; this means that the `BookLister` class depends on it. It cannot carry out its work without a `BookService` implementation. Therefore, `BookLister` has a dependency on the `BookService` interface and on some implementation of it. The `BookLister` class itself instantiates `BookServiceImpl` as its `BookService` implementation. Therefore, the `BookLister` class is said to satisfy its own dependencies. When a class satisfies its own dependencies, it automatically also depends on the classes it satisfies the dependencies with. In this case, `BookLister` now also depends on `BookServiceImpl`, and if any, on the other values passed as a parameter to the `BookServiceImpl` constructor. The `BookService` interface can have many implementations such as Spring JDBC-based data access and JPA-based data access implementation. We cannot use a different implementation of the `BookService` interface without changing the code.

To refactor this tight coupling, we can move the `BookService` instantiation to the constructor of the class. The following is the modified `BookLister` class:

```
public class BookLister {

  private final BookService bookFinder;

  public BookLister(BookService bookFinder) {
    this.bookFinder = bookFinder;
  }

  public List<Book> findByAuthor(String author){
    List<Book> books = new ArrayList<>();

    for(Book aBook:bookFinder.findAll()){
      for(String anAuthor:aBook.getAuthors()){
        if(anAuthor.equals(author)){
          books.add(aBook);
          break;
        }
      }
    }

    return books;
  }

}
```

Note that the `BookService` dependency is passed to the `BookLister` constructor as a constructor argument. Now, `BookLister` is only depending on `BookService`. Whoever instantiates the `BookLister` constructor will satisfy the dependency. The `BookService` dependency is said to be injected into the `BookLister` constructor, hence the term dependency injection. It is now possible to change the `BookService` implementation used by the `BookLister` class without changing the `BookLister` class.

There are two types of dependency injections:

- Constructor injection
- Setter injection

A Spring configuration file creates/defines and configures (resolves dependencies) beans. In the Spring configuration file, the constructor injection is constructed as follows:

```
<bean id="bookLister" class="com.packt.di.BookLister">
  <constructor-arg ref="bookService"/>
</bean>
<bean id="bookService" class="com.packt.di.BookServiceImpl" />
```

The preceding code is equivalent to the following:

```
BookService service = new BookServiceImpl();
BookLister bookLister = new BookLister(service);
```

The setter injection is carried out by setting a property. In a setter injection, instead of passing `bookService` as a constructor argument, we change the class to pass as a setter method argument.

The Spring configuration is as follows:

```
<bean id="bookListerSetterInjection" class="com.packt.di.BookLister">
    <property name="bookService" ref="bookService" />
</bean>

<bean id="bookService" class="com.packt.di.BookServiceImpl" />
```

The preceding code snippet is equivalent to the following:

```
BookService service = new BookServiceImpl();
BookLister bookLister = new BookLister();
bookLister.setBookService(service);
```

The Spring IoC container is known as `ApplicationContext`. The objects that are used in our application, defined in `ApplicationContext`, and managed by the Spring IoC container are called beans; for example, `bookService` is a bean.

A bean is an object that is managed by the Spring IoC container; beans are created with the configuration metadata that you supply to the container, such as in the form of XML `<bean/>` definitions or using Java annotations.

A bean definition describes a bean instance. The bean definition contains the information called configuration metadata, which is needed by the container to know how to create the bean, the life cycle of the bean, and the dependencies of the bean.

The following properties are used to define a bean:

- `class`: This is mandatory and provides the fully qualified bean class name required for the container to create the bean instance.

- `name`: This attribute (also known as `id`) uniquely identifies a bean.

- `scope`: This provides the scope of the objects created from a bean definition, such as `prototype` and `singleton`. We'll learn about them later.

- `constructor-arg`: This injects a dependency as a bean's constructor argument.

- `properties`: This injects a dependency as a setter method argument.

- `lazy-init`: If this is set as `true`, the IoC container creates the bean instance when it is first requested, rather than at startup, which means any configuration error is not discovered until the bean is eventually instantiated inside the Spring context.

- `init-method`: This provides the method name of the bean that is being invoked just after all necessary properties on the bean are set by the IoC container. This is useful when we need to initialize/compute something after the bean is instantiated.

- `destroy-method`: The container calls this method when the bean is destroyed; this is necessary when we need to clean up something before the bean is destroyed.

The following are the bean scopes:

- `singleton`: A single instance of the bean per IoC container. This is not actually the same as in the singleton design pattern (that is, one instance per classloader).

- `prototype`: A single bean definition to have any number of object instances. A new bean instance is created each time one is needed.

- `request`: A bean instance per HTTP request, only valid in the web-aware application context.

- `session`: A bean instance per HTTP session, only valid in the web-aware application context.

- `global-session`: A bean instance per global HTTP session, only valid in the web-aware application context.

The following are the steps in a bean's life cycle:

1. The first step is to find and instantiate the beans. The Spring IoC container reads the bean definitions from the XML and then instantiates them.

2. The next step is to populate the bean properties and satisfy the dependencies. The IoC container uses dependency injection to set the properties.

3. After setting the dependencies, the `setBeanName` method is invoked on the beans; if they implement the `BeanNameAware` interface, the `setBeanName()` method is invoked by passing the ID of the bean.

4. After this, if a bean implements the `BeanFactoryAware` interface, the `setBeanFactory()` method is called with an instance of itself.

5. The pre-initialization of `BeanPostProcessor` is done. If a bean has any `BeanPostProcessor` interface associated with it, the `processBeforeInitialization()` methods are called on the post processors.

6. The init method is called; if a bean specifies an `init-method`, it will be called.

7. Finally, the post-initialization is done; if there are any `BeanPostProcessors` associated with the bean, their `postProcessAfterInitialization()` methods are invoked.

Note that a POJO doesn't need to depend on anything Spring-specific. For particular cases, Spring provides hooks in the form of these interfaces. Using them means introducing a dependency on Spring. The following figure depicts the bean's life cycle:

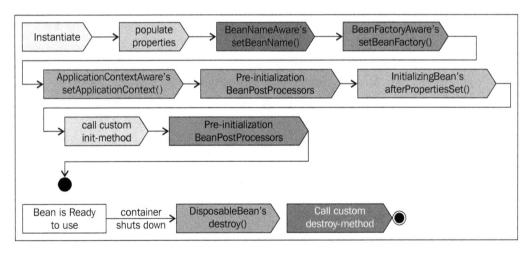

To learn more about DI and IoC, visit the Martin Fowler site at http://martinfowler.com/articles/injection.html.

Printing Hello World

In this section, we'll create a hello world example and set up the Eclipse environment for Spring. You can download the latest Eclipse version from `http://www.eclipse.org/downloads/`.

Note that Spring provides a specific Eclipse distribution for Spring, known as **Spring Tool Suite (STS)**. STS is customized for developing Spring applications. You can download STS from `http://spring.io/tools/sts`.

Download the Spring 4.1.0 JAR from the Maven repository at `http://search.maven.org/` or `http://mvnrepository.com/artifact/org.springframework.`

1. Launch Eclipse and create a Java project and name it `SpringOverview`.

2. Add the following dependencies:

3. Create a `com.packt.lifecycle` package under `src`.

4. Add a `HelloWorld` class with following details:

```java
public class HelloWorld {
  private String message;
  public String getMessage() {
    return message;
  }
}
```

```
public void setMessage(String message) {
  this.message = message;
}
}
```

5. Add an XML file, `applicationContext.xml`, directly under the `src` folder and add the bean definition as follows:

```xml
<?xml version="1.0" encoding="UTF-8"?>
<beans xmlns="http://www.springframework.org/schema/beans"
  xmlns:xsi="http://www.w3.org/2001/XMLSchema-instance"
  xsi:schemaLocation="http://www.springframework.org/schema/beans
http://www.springframework.org/schema/beans/spring-beans.xsd">

  <bean id="helloWorld" class="com.packt.lifecycle.HelloWorld">
    <property name="message" value="Welcome to the Spring world">
    </property>
  </bean>
</beans>
```

6. Create a Java class, `HelloWorldExample`, and add the following lines to check the bean configuration:

```java
public class HelloWorldExample {
  public static void main(String[] args) {
    ApplicationContext context = new
      ClassPathXmlApplicationContext(
        "applicationContext.xml");
    HelloWorld world = (HelloWorld)
      context.getBean("helloWorld");
    System.out.println(world.getMessage());
  }
}
```

We load the Spring bean configuration from an XML file, which is kept in the classpath and named `applicationContext.xml`, and then ask the context to find a bean with a name or ID as `helloWorld`. Finally, we call the `getMessage()` method on the bean to check the value we set in the application context.

7. When we run the `HelloWorldExample` program, the following output is displayed:

```
Sep 07, 2014 4:56:08 PM org.springframework.context.support.AbstractApplicationContext prepareRefresh
INFO: Refreshing org.springframework.context.support.ClassPathXmlApplicationContext@66492ff1: startup date
Sep 07, 2014 4:56:08 PM org.springframework.beans.factory.xml.XmlBeanDefinitionReader loadBeanDefinitions
INFO: Loading XML bean definitions from class path resource [applicationContext.xml]
Welcome to the Spring world
```

Examining life cycle messages

We read about the bean's life cycle; why don't we try to examine the life cycle?

Modify the `HelloWorld` class and implement the following Spring Framework interfaces:

- `ApplicationContextAware`: This will ask you to implement the `setApplicationContext` method

- `BeanNameAware`: This will tell you to implement the `setBeanName` method

- `InitializingBean`: This will force you to implement the `afterPropertiesSet()` method

- `BeanFactoryAware`: This will request you to implement the `setBeanFactory` method

- `BeanPostProcessor`: This needs you to implement the `postProcessBeforeInitialization` and `postProcessAfterInitialization` methods

- `DisposableBean`: This needs to implement the `destroy()` method

Add the `System.out.println` statement in all the implemented methods. Now, add the following two methods:

```
public void myInit() {
   System.out.println("custom myInit is called ");
}

public void myDestroy() {
   System.out.println("custom myDestroy is called ");
}
```

Modify the bean definition to call the `init-method` and `destroy-method` methods. The following is the modified bean definition:

```
<bean id="helloWorld" class="com.packt.lifecycle.HelloWorld"
  init-method="myInit" destroy-method="myDestroy">
  <property name="message" value="Welcome to the Spring world">
  </property>
</bean>
```

Now, modify `HelloWorldExample` to destroy the application context by registering to shutdown hook. The following is the modified code:

```
AbstractApplicationContext context = new  ClassPathXmlApplicationConte
xt("applicationContext.xml");
  HelloWorld world = (HelloWorld) context.getBean("helloWorld");
  System.out.println(world.getMessage());
  context.registerShutdownHook();
```

When we run the application, the following output is displayed:

```
setBeanName is called with helloWorld
setBeanFactory is called
setApplicationContext is called
afterPropertiesSet is called
custom myInit is called
Welcome to the Spring world
destroy is called
custom myDestroy is called
```

Note that the `setBeanName` method is invoked first, then the `setBeanFactory`, `setApplicationContext`, and `afterProperiesSet` methods are called, and then the custom `init` method is invoked. During destruction, the `destroy` method is called first and then the custom `destroy-method` is invoked.

Working with autowiring and annotations

The Spring container can autowire dependencies between the collaborating beans without using the `<constructor-arg>` and `<property>` elements that simplify the application context XML configuration.

The following autowiring modes can be used to instruct a Spring container to use autowiring for dependency injection:

- `no`: By default, the settings is `no`. This means no autowiring.
- `byName`: The container tries to match and wire bean properties with the beans defined by the same name in the configuration file.

- `byType`: The container tries to match a property if its type matches with exactly one of the bean names in the configuration file. If more than one such bean exists, an exception is thrown.

- `constructor`: This is similar to type but looks at the constructor type matching. If more than one bean of the constructor argument type is found in the container, an exception is thrown.

- `default`: This tries to wire using autowire by `constructor`; if it does not work, then it tries autowire by `byType`.

Let's modify our `HelloWorld` example and try wiring by name:

```
<bean name="message" class="java.lang.String">
   <constructor-arg value="auto wired" />
</bean>

<bean id="helloWorld" class="com.packt.lifecycle.HelloWorld"
autowire="byName">
</bean>
```

It will print **auto wired**.

Spring provides annotations to wire collaborators. The following are the annotations:

- `@Required`: This annotation applies to the bean property setter method

- `@Autowired`: This can be applied to bean property setter methods, constructor, and properties

- `@Qualifier`: This annotation along with `@Autowired` can be used to wire a bean with the qualifier name

To enable autowiring through an annotation, the application context needs to be configured to indicate the annotation. Add the following entry to the application context:

```
<context:annotation-config/>
```

Modify the application context to enable an annotation:

```
<?xml version="1.0" encoding="UTF-8"?>
<beans xmlns="http://www.springframework.org/schema/beans"
    xmlns:context="http://www.springframework.org/schema/context"
    xmlns:xsi="http://www.w3.org/2001/XMLSchema-instance"
    xsi:schemaLocation="http://www.springframework.org/schema/beans
http://www.springframework.org/schema/beans/spring-beans.xsd
    http://www.springframework.org/schema/context
```

```
            http://www.springframework.org/schema/context/spring-context-
    3.0.xsd">

    <context:annotation-config/>
        <bean name="message" id="message" class="java.lang.String">
            <constructor-arg value="auto wired" />
        </bean>

        <bean id="helloWorld" class="com.packt.lifecycle.HelloWorld">
        </bean>

    </beans>
```

Modify the `HelloWorld` class to annotate the setter method (`setMessage`) or the private message property with `@Autowired`:

```
    public class HelloWorld implements ApplicationContextAware,BeanNameAwa
    re, InitializingBean,
        BeanFactoryAware,BeanPostProcessor,  DisposableBean {

      private String message;

      public String getMessage() {
        return message;
      }

      @Autowired
      public void setMessage(String message) {
        this.message = message;
      }
        //code omitted for brevity
    }
```

Rerun the application; you will see the **auto wired** message.

Working with aspects

AOP is one of the key components of Spring Framework. Object-oriented programming fails to deal with technical and functional cross-cutting concerns, such as generic functionalities that are needed in many places in our application.

The following are a few examples of cross-cutting concerns:

- Logging and tracing
- Transaction management
- Security
- Caching
- Error handling
- Performance monitoring
- Custom business rules
- Event handling

In our application, we need logging to debug or troubleshoot, so we put debug messages in every method; this is a cross-cutting concern. Similarly, we secure methods for unauthorized access.

AOP overlays a new layer onto the data-driven composition of OOP. This layer corresponds to the cross-cutting functionalities that are difficult to integrate through the OOP paradigm.

AOP is implemented with AspectJ and Spring AOP:

- **AspectJ**: This is the original AOP technology (the first version dates from 1995) that offers a full-blown, aspect-oriented programming language and uses bytecode modification for aspect weaving.
- **Spring AOP**: This is a Java-based AOP framework and it uses dynamic proxies for aspect weaving. This focuses on using AOP to solve enterprise problems.

The following example demonstrates a cross-cutting concern:

```
class Account{
  private double balance;
  public void withdraw(double amount){
    logger.debug("Withdraw -"+amount);
    tx.begin();
      balance = this.balance-amount;
      accountDao.saveBalance(balance);
    tx.commit();
  }
}
```

The `withdraw` method logs debug information, begins a transaction, performs a database transaction, and finally commits the transaction. In each method, we will introduce duplicate code for debugging and opening and committing a transaction. These are cross-cutting concerns as the conceptually duplicate code will be scattered to all modules in the application. This is bad in the sense that if we need to change any settings, we have to manually change all methods in all modules, such as instead of `logger.debug`, and if we need to change the logging to `logger.info`, we need to modify all methods.

Before we dig deep into AOP, let's get familiar with the terminology:

- **Join point**: This is a well-defined point during the execution of your application. You can insert additional logic at join points.

  Examples of join points are as follows:

  - Method invocation
  - Class initialization
  - Object initialization

- **Advice**: This is the code that is executed at a specific join point. The three types of advice are as follows:

  - The before advice is executed before a join point.
  - The after advice is executed after a join point.
  - The around advice is executed around a join point. The around advice spans the before and after advice.

- **Pointcut**: This is a collection of join points to execute an advice. A join point is a possibility of executing an advice, whereas a pointcut is a set of selected join points where actually the advice is executed.

- **Aspect**: This defines the implementation of the cross-cutting concern. An aspect is the combination of advice and pointcuts. An application can have any number of aspects, depending on the requirement.

- **Weaving**: This is the process of applying aspects into the code at the appropriate join points. There are three types of weaving:

  - Compile-time weaving
  - Class load-time weaving
  - Runtime weaving

- **Target**: This is the object that is advised by one or more aspects.
- **Introduction**: This is the process by which you can modify the structure of an object by introducing additional methods or fields to it. You use the introduction to make any object implement a specific interface without needing the object's class to implement that interface explicitly.

There are two types of AOP:

- Static AOP
    - The weaving process forms another step in the build process for an application
    - For example, in a Java program, you can achieve the weaving process by modifying the actual bytecode of the application by changing and modifying the code as necessary

- Dynamic AOP
    - The weaving process is performed dynamically at runtime
    - It is easy to change the weaving process without recompilation

Spring AOP is based on proxies. To know more about proxies, read about the proxy pattern or visit http://en.wikipedia.org/wiki/Proxy_pattern.

We'll display Hello World! through AOP. The following are the steps to create the hello world message:

1. Create an interface called IMessageWriter:

```
package com.packt.aop;

public interface IMessageWriter {
  void writeMessage();
}
```

2. Create a class called MessageWriter and implement the IMessageWriter interface:

```
package com.packt.aop;

public class MessageWriter implements IMessageWriter {

  @Override
  public void writeMessage() {
    System.out.print("World");
  }

}
```

3. The join point is the invocation of the `writeMessage()` method. What we need is an around advice as we'll prepend `Hello` before `World` and append the exclamation after `World` to make it `Hello World !`. The `MethodInterceptor` interface is AOP Alliance standard interface for around interface. The `MethodInvocation` object represents the method invocation that is being advised. We'll create an advice as follows:

```java
import org.aopalliance.intercept.MethodInterceptor;
import org.aopalliance.intercept.MethodInvocation;
public class MessageDecorator implements MethodInterceptor {
  public Object invoke(MethodInvocation invocation)
    throws Throwable {
    System.out.print("Hello ");
    Object retVal = invocation.proceed();
    System.out.println("!");
    return retVal;
  }
}
```

4. We'll use the `ProxyFactory` class to create the proxy of the target object:

```java
import org.springframework.aop.framework.ProxyFactory;

public class AOPTest {

  public static void main(String[] args) {
    MessageWriter target = new MessageWriter();
    // create the proxy
    ProxyFactory pf = new ProxyFactory();
    // Add the given AOP Alliance advice to the tail
    // of the advice (interceptor) chain
    pf.addAdvice(new MessageDecorator());
    // Set the given object as target
    pf.setTarget(target);
    // Create a new proxy according to the
    // settings in this factory
    MessageWriter proxy = (MessageWriter)
        pf.getProxy();
    // write the messages
    target.writeMessage();
    System.out.println("");
    // use the proxy
    proxy.writeMessage();
  }
}
```

When we run the program, the MessageDecorator around advice is applied on the proxy object. When proxy.writeMessage is called, the correct output is displayed.

Exploring Spring JDBC

The **Spring Data Access Object (DAO)** support makes it easy to work with data access technologies such as JDBC, Hibernate, or JDO in a standardized way. Spring Framework provides APIs to reduce JDBC code duplication. Spring JDBC hides the low-level details and allows us to concentrate on business logic, which makes switching between databases easy and simple.

In a normal JDBC code, we catch a series of checked exceptions such as SQLException while acquiring a connection or executing a SQL statement; with Spring, we can code without worrying about catching exceptions, as Spring does the exception handling for us. Spring is not throwing away or eating the checked exceptions but is instead translating them to unchecked/runtime ones.

Spring provides a set of abstract DAO classes that one can extend; these abstract classes have methods to provide the data source and any other configuration settings that are specific to the technology one is currently using.

The following are the DAO support classes:

* JdbcDaoSupport
* HibernateDaoSupport
* JdoDaoSupport
* JpaDaoSupport

In normal JDBC code, we write the code in the following way to access the database:

1. Define the connection parameters.
2. Open the connection.
3. Specify the statement.
4. Prepare and execute the statement.
5. Set up the loop to iterate through the results (if any).
6. Do the work for each iteration.
7. Process any exception.
8. Handle transactions.
9. Close the connection.

Spring Framework relaxes the requirement to write numerous JDBC code lines. We need to write only the code to perform the following:

- Specify the statement
- Do the work for each iteration

Spring takes care of all the grungy, low-level details that can make JDBC such a tedious API to develop against.

The Spring-JDBC abstraction framework consists of four different packages:

- `org.springframework.jdbc.core`
- `org.springframework.jdbc.datasource`
- `org.springframework.jdbc.object`
- `org.springframework.jdbc.support`

The `org.springframework.jdbc.core` package contains the following:

- The `JdbcTemplate` class
- Various callback interfaces
- A variety of related classes

The `org.springframework.jdbc.datasource` package contains the following classes:

- A utility class for easy `DataSource` access
- Various simple `DataSource` implementations that can be used to test and run unmodified JDBC code outside of a J2EE container
- The utility class provides static methods to obtain connections from JNDI and to close connections if necessary
- It has support for thread-bound connections, for example, to use with `DataSourceTransactionManager`

The `org.springframework.jdbc.object` package contains the following:

- Classes that represent RDBMS queries, updates, and stored procedures as thread-safe, reusable objects
- This approach is modeled by JDO, although of course, objects returned by queries are disconnected from the database
- This higher level of JDBC abstraction depends on the lower-level abstraction in the `org.springframework.jdbc.core` package

The `org.springframework.jdbc.support` package contains the following:

- The `SQLException` translation functionality and some utility classes
- Exceptions thrown during JDBC processing are translated to exceptions defined in the `org.springframework.dao` package
- The code using the Spring JDBC abstraction layer does not need to implement JDBC-or RDBMS-specific error handling
- All translated exceptions are unchecked giving you the option of catching the exceptions that you can recover from while allowing other exceptions to be propagated to the caller

The `JdbcTemplate` class is the main class in the `org.springframework.jdbc.core` package. It simplifies the use of JDBC since it handles the creation and release of resources. This helps avoid common errors such as not closing the connection, and it executes the core JDBC workflow such as statement creation and execution leaving application code to provide SQL and extract results.

We'll build a phone book application and store phone numbers using Spring JDBC and normal JDBC and realize the simplicity and usability of Spring JDBC. We'll use the Apache Derby database for persistence. Derby can be downloaded from `http://db.apache.org/derby/`.

You can use better built-in databases such as H2. It has more features and less restriction than Derby. However, we're using Derby for simplicity.

The following are the steps to run Derby:

1. Download the binary media file and extract media to a location. We'll refer to it as DERBY_HOME in the next steps.
2. On a Windows machine, go to DERBY_HOME\bin and execute `startNetworkServer.bat`.
3. It will launch Command Prompt and print to the console that the database server is started, such as the following:

   `started and ready to accept connections on port 1527.`

Download the latest version of the Spring JDBC JAR and its dependencies from `http://maven.springframework.org/release/org/springframework/spring/`.

Perform the following steps to implement Spring JDBC and simplify the code:

1. Launch Eclipse and create a Java project named `DatabaseAccess`.

2. Add a class `PhoneEntry` to store phone details. The following are the class details:

```
package com.packt.database.model;

public class PhoneEntry implements Serializable {

private static final long serialVersionUID = 1L;

private String phoneNumber;
private String firstName;
private String lastName;

// getters and setters
}
```

3. Create a data access interface for the phone book. The following are the API details:

```
package com.packt.database.dao;

import java.util.List;
import com.packt.database.model.PhoneEntry;

public interface PhoneBookDao {
  boolean create(PhoneEntry entry);

  boolean update(PhoneEntry entryToUpdate);

  List<PhoneEntry> searchByNumber(String number);

  List<PhoneEntry> searchByFirstName(String firstName);

  List<PhoneEntry> searchByLastName(String lastName);

  boolean delete(String number);
}
```

4. Edit `.classpath` to add the following Spring dependencies:

```
commons-lang-2.3.jar - DatabaseAccess
commons-logging.jar - DatabaseAccess
derby.jar - DatabaseAccess
junit-4.11.jar - DatabaseAccess
mockito-all-1.9.0.jar - DatabaseAccess
org.springframework.asm-3.1.1.RELEASE.jar - DatabaseAccess
org.springframework.beans-3.1.1.RELEASE.jar - DatabaseAccess
org.springframework.core-3.1.1.RELEASE.jar - DatabaseAccess
org.springframework.jdbc-3.1.1.RELEASE.jar - DatabaseAccess
org.springframework.transaction-3.1.1.RELEASE.jar - DatabaseAccess
```

5. Create a database access interface implementation to communicate with the database. The following are the data access object details:

```java
public class PhoneBookDerbyDao implements PhoneBookDao {

    private String driver =
        "org.apache.derby.jdbc.EmbeddedDriver";
    private String protocol = "jdbc:derby:";
    private String userId = "dbo";
    private String dbName = "phoneBook";

    public PhoneBookDerbyDao() {
        loadDriver();
    }

    protected void loadDriver() {
        try {
            Class.forName(driver).newInstance();
        } catch (ClassNotFoundException cnfe) {
            cnfe.printStackTrace(System.err);
        } catch (InstantiationException ie) {
            ie.printStackTrace(System.err);
        } catch (IllegalAccessException iae) {
            iae.printStackTrace(System.err);
        }
    }

    protected Connection getConnection() throws SQLException {
        Connection conn = null;
        Properties props = new Properties();
        props.put("user", userId);
```

```
        conn = DriverManager.getConnection(protocol + dbName +
          ";create=true",props);
        conn.setAutoCommit(false);
        return conn;
    }
}
```

Note that the `PhoneBookDerbyDao` class is a `derby` implementation of the DAO. It has configuration attributes such as `driver`, `protocol`, and `dbName`, and getters/setters. The `loadDriver()` method loads the database driver and gets invoked from the `PhoneBookDerbyDao` constructor. The `getConnection()` method connects to a Derby database and establishes a connection.

6. Implement the `create` behavior:

```
@Override
public boolean create(PhoneEntry entry) {
    PreparedStatement preparedStmt = null;
    Connection conn = null;
    try {
    conn = getConnection();
    preparedStmt = conn
      .prepareStatement("insert into PhoneBook values
            (?,?,?)");

    preparedStmt.setString(1, entry.getPhoneNumber());
    preparedStmt.setString(2, entry.getFirstName());
    preparedStmt.setString(3, entry.getLastName());
    preparedStmt.executeUpdate();
    // Note that it can cause problems on some dbs if
    //autocommit mode is on
    conn.commit();
      return true;
    } catch (SQLException e) {
      e.printStackTrace();
    } finally {

      if (preparedStmt != null) {
        try {
          preparedStmt.close();
        } catch (SQLException e) {
          e.printStackTrace();
        }
      }
```

```
      if (conn != null) {
        try {
          conn.close();
        } catch (SQLException e) {
          e.printStackTrace();
        }
      }
    }

    return false;
  }
```

The `create` method first acquires a database connection and creates a prepared statement from `connection`; it then populates the prepared statement with the `PhoneEntry` values, executes the prepared statement, and then commits the connection. The `finally` block closes the resources, which closes the prepared statement and the connection.

7. Create a class named `PhoneBookDerbySpringDao` that implements the `PhoneBookDao` interface. The following is the Spring implementation of the `create` method:

```
public class PhoneBookDerbySpringDao  implements
    PhoneBookDao {

private final JdbcTemplate jdbcTemplate;

  public PhoneBookDerbySpringDao(JdbcTemplate jdbcTemplate) {
  this.jdbcTemplate = jdbcTemplate;
  }

  @Override
  public boolean create(PhoneEntry entry) {
    int rowCount = jdbcTemplate.update("insert into
            PhoneBook values (?,?,?)",
            new Object[]{entry.getPhoneNumber(),
            entry.getFirstName(),
            entry.getLastName()
      });
    return rowCount == 1;
  }
}
```

The `JdbcTemplate` class simplifies the use of JDBC; it handles the resources and helps avoid common errors such as not closing the connection. It creates and populates the statement object, iterates through `ResultSet`, leaving the application code to provide SQL and extract results. `PhoneBookDerbySpringDao` contains a `JdbcTemplate` instance and delegates the database tasks to `jdbcTemplate`. `JdbcTemplate` uses data source definition from the `applicationContext` file.

`JdbcTemplate` has an `update` method for the insert and update operations. It takes a SQL query and parameters. The new Spring version of the `create()` method invokes the `update()` method on `jdbcTemplate` and passes the `PhoneEntry` details. Now the `create` method looks simple; it is just two lines of code. Spring Framework handles the resource life cycle.

Look at the Spring DAO class; it has only 54 lines. The class looks neat, simple, and readable. It doesn't handle resources; rather, it concentrates on data access.

Handling a transaction with Spring

Spring Framework provides supports for transaction management. The following are characteristics of the Spring transaction management framework:

- Offers abstraction for transaction management
- Defines a programming model that supports different transaction APIs, such as JDBC, JTA, and JPA
- Declarative transaction management is supported
- Provides a simpler programmatic transaction management API
- Easily integrates with Spring's data access abstractions

Two transaction management options are available for the J2EE developers. The following are the two options:

- The application server manages global transactions, using the **Java Transaction API (JTA)**. It supports multiple transaction resources, such as database transactions, JMS transactions, and XA transactions.
- Resource-specific local transactions, such as a transaction associated with a JDBC connection.

Both transaction models have downsides. The global transaction needs an application server and JNDI to manage transactions; it uses JTA but the JTA API is cumbersome and has a complex exception model. The need for an application server, JNDI, and JTA limits the reusability of code.

The local transactions have the following disadvantages:

- Cannot handle multiple transactional resources
- Invasive to the programming model

Spring's transaction model solves the problems associated with the global and local transactions, and it offers a consistent programming model for developers that can be used in any environment.

Spring Framework supports both declarative and programmatic transaction management. Declarative transaction management is the recommended one, and it has been well accepted by the development community.

The programmatic transaction model provides an abstraction that can be run over any underlying transaction infrastructure. The concept of transaction strategy is the key to the transaction abstraction. The org.springframework.transaction. PlatformTransactionManager interface defines the strategy.

The following is the PlatformTransactionManager interface:

```
public interface PlatformTransactionManager {
    TransactionStatus getTransaction(
    TransactionDefinition definition) throws TransactionException;
    void commit(TransactionStatus status) throws
                                      TransactionException;
    void rollback(TransactionStatus status) throws
                                      TransactionException;
}
```

The following are the characteristics of PlatformTransactionManager:

- PlatformTransactionManager is not a class; instead, it is an interface, and thus it can be easily mocked or stubbed to write tests.
- It doesn't need a JNDI lookup strategy, as its implementations can be defined as Spring beans in Spring Framework's IoC container.
- Methods defined in PlatformTransactionManager throw TransactionException. However, this is an unchecked exception, so programmers are not forced to handle the exception. But in reality, the exception is fatal in nature; when it is thrown, there is very little chance that the failure can be recovered.
- The getTransaction() method takes a TransactionDefinition parameter and returns a TransactionStatus object. The TransactionStatus object can be a new or an existing transaction.

The `TransactionDefinition` interface defines the following:

```
public interface TransactionDefinition {
    int getIsolationLevel();
    int getPropagationBehavior();
    String getName();
    int getTimeout();
    boolean isReadOnly();
}
```

- **Isolation**: This returns the degree of isolation of this transaction from other transactions. The following are the Spring propagations:
  - `ISOLATION_DEFAULT`
  - `ISOLATION_READ_COMMITTED`
  - `ISOLATION_READ_UNCOMMITTED`
  - `ISOLATION_REPEATABLE_READ`
  - `ISOLATION_SERIALIZABLE`

- **Propagation**: This returns the transaction propagation behavior. The following are the allowable values:
  - `PROPAGATION_MANDATORY`: This needs a current transaction and raises an error if no current transaction exists
  - `PROPAGATION_NESTED`: This executes the current transaction within a nested transaction
  - `PROPAGATION_NEVER`: This doesn't support a current transaction and raises an error if a current transaction exists
  - `PROPAGATION_NOT_SUPPORTED`: This executes code non-transactionally
  - `PROPAGATION_REQUIRED`: This creates a new transaction if no transaction exists
  - `PROPAGATION_REQUIRES_NEW`: This suspends the current transaction and creates a new transaction
  - `PROPAGATION_SUPPORTS`: If the current transaction exists, then this supports it; otherwise, it executes the code non-transactionally
  - `TIMEOUT_DEFAULT`: This uses the default timeout

- **Timeout**: This returns the maximum time in seconds that the current transaction should take; if the transaction takes more than that, then the transaction gets rolled back automatically.

- **Read-only status**: This returns whether the transaction is a read-only transaction. A read-only transaction does not modify any data.

The `TransactionStatus` interface provides a simple way for transactional code to control the transaction execution and query the transaction status; it has the following signature:

```
public interface TransactionStatus {
    boolean isNewTransaction();
    void setRollbackOnly();
    boolean isRollbackOnly();
}
```

The `PlatformTransactionManager` implementations normally require knowledge of the environment in which they work, such as JDBC, JTA, Hibernate, and so on.

A local `PlatformTransactionManager` implementation defines a JDBC data source and then uses the Spring `DataSourceTransactionManager` class, which gives it a reference to `DataSource`. The following Spring context defines a local transaction manager:

```
<bean id="dataSource" class="org.apache.commons.dbcp.BasicDataSource"
destroy-method="close">
  <property name="driverClassName" value="${jdbc.driverClassName}" />
  <property name="url" value="${jdbc.url}" />
  <property name="username" value="${jdbc.username}" />
  <property name="password" value="${jdbc.password}" />
</bean>
```

Here, `${jdbc.xxxx}` represents the values defined in the properties file. Usually, the convention is that the JDBC properties are defined in a properties file that is then loaded from `applicationContext`, and then the JDBC properties are accessed using the key such as `${key}`. The following is the XML configuration of transaction manager:

```
<bean id="txManager" class="org.springframework.jdbc.datasource.
DataSourceTransactionManager">
  <property name="dataSource" ref="dataSource"/>
</bean>
```

When we use JTA in a J2EE container and use a container `DataSource` obtained via the JNDI lookup, in conjunction with Spring's `JtaTransactionManager`, then `JtaTransactionManager` doesn't need to know about `DataSource`, or any other specific resources, as it will use the container's global transaction management infrastructure.

The following is the `JtaTransactionManager` definition in Spring context:

```
<jee:jndi-lookup id="dataSource" jndi-name="myDataSource "/>
<bean id="txManager" class="org.springframework.transaction.jta.
JtaTransactionManager"/>
```

The benefit of Spring transaction manager is that in all cases, the application code will not need to change at all. We can change how transactions are managed merely by changing the configuration, even if that change means moving from local to global transactions or vice versa.

Declarative transaction management is preferred by most users; it is the option with the least impact on the application code. It is most consistent with the ideals of a non-invasive lightweight container. Spring's declarative transaction management is made possible with Spring AOP.

The similarities between the EJB CMT and Spring declarative transaction are as follows:

- It is possible to specify transaction behavior down to the individual method level
- It is possible to make a `setRollbackOnly()` call within a transaction context if necessary

Working with declarative Spring transaction

We'll create a simple Spring transaction management project and learn about the basics. The following are the steps to create the project:

1. Create an empty class, `Foo`, under the `com.packt.tx` package. The following is the class body:

```
package com.packt.tx;

public class Foo {

}
```

2. Create an interface, `FooService`, to handle the CRUD operations on `Foo`:

```
package com.packt.tx;

public interface FooService {

    Foo getFoo(String fooName);

    void insertFoo(Foo foo);

    void updateFoo(Foo foo);

}
```

3. Create a default implementation of `FooService`, and from each method, throw `UnsupportedOperationException` to impersonate a rollback transaction:

```
public class FooServiceImpl implements FooService {

    @Override
    public Foo getFoo(String fooName) {
        throw new UnsupportedOperationException();
    }
    @Override
    public void insertFoo(Foo foo) {
        throw new UnsupportedOperationException();

    }
    @Override
    public void updateFoo(Foo foo) {
        throw new UnsupportedOperationException();

    }

}
```

4. Create an application context file called `applicationContextTx.xml` directly under the `src` folder and add the following entries:

    Define the `fooService` bean:

```
<bean id="fooService" class="com.packt.tx.FooServiceImpl" />
```

    Define a Derby data source:

```
<bean id="dataSource" class="org.apache.commons.dbcp2.
BasicDataSource"
    destroy-method="close">
```

```xml
        <property name="driverClassName" value="org.apache.derby.jdbc.
EmbeddedDriver" />
        <property name="url" value="jdbc:derby:derbyDB;create=true" />
        <property name="username" value="dbo" />
        <property name="password" value="" />
    </bean>
```

Define a transaction manager with the data source:

```xml
<bean id="txManager"
    class="org.springframework.jdbc.datasource.
      DataSourceTransactionManager">
    <property name="dataSource" ref="dataSource" />
</bean>
```

Define an advice with transaction manager so that all get methods will have a read-only transaction:

```xml
<tx:advice id="txAdvice" transaction-manager="txManager">
    <tx:attributes>
    <!--all methods starting with 'get' are read-only-->
      <tx:method name="get*" read-only="true" />
      <tx:method name="*" />
    </tx:attributes>
  </tx:advice>
```

Define the AOP configuration to apply the advice on pointcut:

```xml
  <aop:config>
    <aop:pointcut id="fooServiceOperation"
      expression="execution(* com.packt.tx.FooService.*(..))" />
    <aop:advisor advice-ref="txAdvice" pointcut-
ref="fooServiceOperation" />
  </aop:config>
</beans>
```

5. Create a test class to get the FooService bean and call the getFoo method on the FooService bean. The following is the class:

```java
public class TransactionTest {

  public static void main(String[] args) {
    AbstractApplicationContext context = new
      ClassPathXmlApplicationContext(
        "applicationContextTx.xml");

    FooService fooService = (FooService)
      context.getBean("fooService");
```

```
System.out.println(fooService);
fooService.getFoo(null);
    }
}
```

6. When we run the program, Spring creates a transaction and then rolls back the transaction as it throws UnsupportedOperationException. Check the log to get the details. The following is the log:

```
- Creating new transaction with name [com.packt.tx.FooServiceImpl.
getFoo]: PROPAGATION_REQUIRED,ISOLATION_DEFAULT,readOnly
- Acquired Connection [341280385, URL=jdbc:derby:derbyDB,
UserName=dbo, Apache Derby Embedded JDBC Driver] for JDBC
transaction
- Setting JDBC Connection [341280385, URL=jdbc:derby:derbyDB,
UserName=dbo, Apache Derby Embedded JDBC Driver] read-only
- Switching JDBC Connection [341280385, URL=jdbc:derby:derbyDB,
UserName=dbo, Apache Derby Embedded JDBC Driver] to manual commit
- Bound value [org.springframework.jdbc.datasource.
ConnectionHolder@6b58ba2b] for key [org.apache.commons.dbcp2.
BasicDataSource@680624c7] to thread [main]
- Initializing transaction synchronization
- Getting transaction for [com.packt.tx.FooServiceImpl.getFoo]
- Completing transaction for [com.packt.tx.FooServiceImpl.getFoo]
after exception: java.lang.UnsupportedOperationException
- Applying rules to determine whether transaction should rollback
on java.lang.UnsupportedOperationException
- Winning rollback rule is: null
- No relevant rollback rule found: applying default rules
- Triggering beforeCompletion synchronization
- Initiating transaction rollback
- Rolling back JDBC transaction on Connection [341280385,
URL=jdbc:derby:derbyDB, UserName=dbo, Apache Derby Embedded JDBC
Driver]
```

Exploring transaction attributes

We declared a transaction advice and its attributes in the preceding example. This section examines the transaction attributes such as propagation, isolation, read-only, timeout, and rollback rules.

Transaction propagation has seven levels:

- PROPAGATION_MANDATORY: Method should run in a transaction and if nothing exists, an exception will be thrown.

- PROPAGATION_NESTED: Method should run in a nested transaction.

- `PROPAGATION_NEVER`: The current method should not run in a transaction. If this exists, an exception will be thrown.

- `PROPAGATION_NOT_SUPPORTED`: Method should not run in a transaction. The existing transaction will be suspended till the method completes the execution.

- `PROPAGATION_REQUIRED`: Method should run in a transaction. If this already exists, the method will run in that, and if not, a new transaction will be created.

- `PROPAGATION_REQUIRES_NEW`: Method should run in a new transaction. If this already exists, it will be suspended till the method finishes.

- `PROPAGATION_SUPPORTS`: Method need not run in a transaction. If this already exists, it supports one that is already in progress.

The following are the isolation levels:

- `ISOLATION_DEFAULT`: This is the default isolation specific to the data source.

- `ISOLATION_READ_UNCOMMITTED`: This reads changes that are uncommitted. This leads to dirty reads, phantom reads, and non-repeatable reads.

  A dirty read happens when a transaction is allowed to read data from a row that has been modified by another running transaction and not yet committed.

  Data getting changed in the current transaction by other transactions is known as a phantom read.

  A non-repeatable read means data that is read twice inside the same transaction cannot be guaranteed to contain the same value.

- `ISOLATION_READ_COMMITTED`: This reads only committed data. Dirty reads are prevented but repeatable and non-repeatable reads are possible.

- `ISOLATION_REPEATABLE_READ`: Multiple reads of the same field yield the same results unless modified by the same transaction. Dirty and non-repeatable reads are prevented but phantom reads are possible as other transactions can edit the fields.

- `ISOLATION_SERIALIZABLE`: Dirty, phantom, and non-repeatable reads are prevented. However, this hampers the performance of the application.

The read-only attribute specifies that the transaction is only going to read data from a database. It can be applied to only those propagation settings that start a transaction, that is, `PROPAGATION_REQUIRED`, `PROPAGATION_REQUIRES_NEW`, and `PROPAGATION_NESTED`.

The timeout specifies the maximum time allowed for a transaction to run. This is required for the transactions that run for very long and hold locks for a long time. When a transaction reaches the timeout period, it is rolled back. The timeout needs to be specified only on propagation settings that start a new transaction.

We can specify that transactions will roll back on certain exceptions and do not roll back on other exceptions by specifying the rollback rules.

Using the @Transactional annotation

The functionality offered by the @Transactional annotation and the support classes is only available in Java 5 (Tiger) and above. The @Transactional annotation can be placed before an interface definition, a method on an interface, a class definition, or a public method on a class. A method in the same class takes precedence over the transactional settings defined in the class-level annotation.

The following example demonstrates the method-level precedence:

```
@Transactional(readOnly = true)
public class FooServiceImpl implements FooService {
    public Foo getFoo(String fooName) {

    }
    // This settings has precedence for this method
    @Transactional(readOnly = false, propagation =
      Propagation.REQUIRES_NEW)
    public void updateFoo(Foo foo) {
    }
}
```

However, the mere presence of the @Transactional annotation is not enough to actually turn on the transactional behavior; the @Transactional annotation is simply metadata that can be consumed by something that is aware of @Transactional and that can use the metadata to configure the appropriate beans with the transactional behavior.

The default @Transactional settings are as follows:

- The propagation setting is PROPAGATION_REQUIRED
- The isolation level is ISOLATION_DEFAULT
- The transaction is read/write

- The transaction timeout defaults to the default timeout of the underlying transaction system, or none if timeouts are not supported

- Any `RuntimeException` will trigger a rollback and any checked exception will not trigger a rollback

When the previous POJO is defined as a bean in a Spring IoC container, the bean instance can be made transactional by adding one line of XML configuration. We'll examine the `@Transactional` annotation in the following example:

1. Create a application context file called `applicationContextTxAnnotation. xml` and add the following lines (no need for `aop` and `advice`):

```xml
<context:annotation-config />
<bean id="fooService" class="com.packt.tx.FooServiceImpl" />

<!-- enable the configuration of transactional behavior based on
annotations -->
<tx:annotation-driven transaction-manager="txManager" />

<bean id="dataSource"
  class="org.apache.commons.dbcp2.BasicDataSource"
    destroy-method="close">
    <property name="driverClassName"
    value="org.apache.derby.jdbc.EmbeddedDriver" />
    <property name="url"
    value="jdbc:derby:derbyDB;create=true" />
    <property name="username" value="dbo" />
    <property name="password" value="" />
</bean>

<bean id="txManager"
  class="org.springframework.jdbc.datasource
    .DataSourceTransactionManager">
    <property name="dataSource" ref="dataSource" />
</bean>
```

2. Annotate `FooServiceImpl` with the `@Transactional` annotation:

```java
@Transactional
public class FooServiceImpl implements FooService {

  @Override public Foo getFoo(String fooName) {
    throw new UnsupportedOperationException();
  }
```

```
@Override public void insertFoo(Foo foo) {
  throw new UnsupportedOperationException();
    }

@Override public void updateFoo(Foo foo) {
  throw new UnsupportedOperationException();
  }
}
```

3. Create a class called `TransactionTestAnnotation`, load `applicationContextTxAnnotation`, and examine whether the same log appears. The following is the class:

```
public class TransactionTestAnnotation {

  public static void main(String[] args) {
    AbstractApplicationContext context = new
    ClassPathXmlApplicationContext(
      "applicationContextTxAnnotation.xml");

    FooService fooService = (FooService)
      context.getBean("fooService");
    System.out.println(fooService);
    fooService.getFoo(null);
  }
}
```

Working with a programmatic Spring transaction

Spring provides two means of programmatic transaction management:

*   Using `TransactionTemplate`
*   Using a `PlatformTransactionManager` implementation directly

The Spring team generally recommends the first approach (using `TransactionTemplate`).

The second approach is similar to using the JTA `UserTransaction` API (although exception handling is less cumbersome).

Using TransactionTemplate

The following are the characteristics of TransactionTemplate:

- It adopts the same approach as other Spring templates such as JdbcTemplate and HibernateTemplate

- It uses a callback approach

- A TransactionTemplate instance is threadsafe

The following code snippet demonstrates TransactionTemplate with a callback:

```
Object result = transTemplate.execute(new TransactionCallback() {
    public Object doInTransaction(TransactionStatus status) {
        updateOperation();
        return resultOfUpdateOperation();
    }
});
```

If there is no return value, use the convenient TransactionCallbackWithoutResult class via an anonymous class, as follows:

```
transTemplate.execute(new TransactionCallbackWithoutResult() {
protected void doInTransactionWithoutResult(
                            TransactionStatus status) {
        updateOperation1();
        updateOperation2();
    }
});
```

Application classes wishing to use TransactionTemplate must have access to PlatformTransactionManager, which will typically be supplied to the class via a dependency injection. It is easy to unit test such classes with a mock or stub PlatformTransactionManager. There is no JNDI lookup here; it is a simple interface. As usual, you can use Spring to greatly simplify your unit testing.

Using PlatformTransactionManager

A PlatformTransactionManager implementation can be directly used to manage a transaction:

1. Simply pass the implementation of the PlatformTransactionManager to your bean via a bean reference.

2. Then, using the TransactionDefinition and TransactionStatus objects, you can initiate transactions and perform a rollback or commit.

The following code snippet provides an example of such use:

```
DefaultTransactionDefinition def = new DefaultTransactionDefinition();
def.setPropagationBehavior(TransactionDefinition.PROPAGATION_
REQUIRED);
TransactionStatus status = txManager.getTransaction(def);
try {
    // execute your business logic here
} catch (Exception ex) {
    txManager.rollback(status);
    throw ex;
}
txManager.commit(status);
```

Downloading the example code

You can download the example code files for all Packt books you have purchased from your account at http://www.packtpub.com. If you purchased this book elsewhere, you can visit http://www.packtpub.com/support and register to have the files e-mailed directly to you.

Building an MVC application with Spring

The **Model View Controller (MVC)** is a widely used web development pattern. The MVC pattern defines three interconnected components, namely model, view, and controller.

The model represents the application data, logic, or business rules.

The view is a representation of information or a model. A model can have multiple views, for example, marks of a student can be represented in a tabular format or graphical chart.

The controller accepts client requests and initiates commands to either update the model or change the view.

The controller controls the flow of the application. In JEE applications, a controller is usually implemented as a servlet. A controller servlet intercepts requests and then maps each request to an appropriate handler resource. In this section, we will build a classic MVC front controller servlet to redirect requests to views.

Spring MVC is a web application framework that takes advantage of Spring design principles:

- Dependency injection
- Interface-driven design
- POJO without being tied up with a framework

Spring MVC is used for the following advantages:

- Testing through dependency injection
- Binding of request data to domain objects
- Form validation
- Error handling
- Multiple view technologies
- Supports different formats such as JSP, Velocity, Excel, and PDF
- Page workflow

In Spring MVC, the following is a simplified request-handling mechanism:

1. `DispatcherServlet` receives a request and confers with handler mappings to find out which controller can handle the request, and it then passes the request to that controller

2. The controller performs the business logic (can delegate the request to a service or business logic processor) and returns some information back to `DispatcherServlet` for user display/response. Instead of sending the information (model) directly to the user, the controller returns a view name that can render the model.

3. `DispatcherServlet` then resolves the physical view from the view name and passes the model object to the view. This way `DispatcherServlet` is decoupled from the view implementation.

4. The view renders the model. A view can be a JSP page, a servlet, a PDF file, an Excel report, or any presentable component.

The following sequence diagram represents the flow and interaction of Spring MVC components:

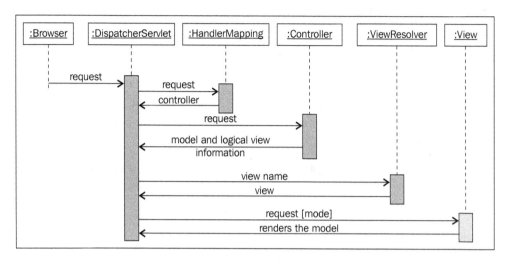

We will build a Spring web application and unit test code using JUnit by performing the following steps:

1. Launch Eclipse and create a dynamic web project called `SpringMvcTest`.

2. Open `web.xml` and enter the following lines:

```xml
<display-name>SpringMVCTest</display-name>
<servlet>
    <servlet-name>dispatcher</servlet-name>
    <servlet-class>
            org.springframework.web.servlet.DispatcherServlet
        </servlet-class>
    <load-on-startup>1</load-on-startup>
</servlet>
<servlet-mapping>
    <servlet-name>dispatcher</servlet-name>
    <url-pattern>/</url-pattern>
</servlet-mapping>
<context-param>
    <param-name>contextConfigLocation</param-name>
    <param-value>
        /WEB-INF/dispatcher-servlet.xml
    </param-value>
</context-param>
</web-app>
```

The dispatcher is a `DispatcherServlet` and it maps all requests. Note the `contextConfigLocation` parameter. This indicates that the Spring beans are defined in `/WEB-INF/dispatcher-servlet.xml`.

3. Create an XML file called `dispatcher-servlet.xml` in `WEB-INF` and add the following lines:

```
<?xml version="1.0" encoding="UTF-8"?>
<beans xmlns="http://www.springframework.org/schema/beans"
  xmlns:context="http://www.springframework.org/schema/context"
xmlns:xsi="http://www.w3.org/2001/XMLSchema-instance"
xsi:schemaLocation="
    http://www.springframework.org/schema/beans
    http://www.springframework.org/schema/beans/spring-beans-
3.0.xsd
    http://www.springframework.org/schema/context
          http://www.springframework.org/schema/context/spring-
context-3.0.xsd">
  <context:component-scan base-package="com.packt" />
  <bean class= "org.springframework.web.servlet.view.
                     InternalResourceViewResolver">
    <property name="prefix">
      <value>/WEB-INF/pages/</value>
    </property>
    <property name="suffix">
      <value>.jsp</value>
    </property>
</bean>
```

This XML defines a Spring view resolver. Any view will be found under the `/WEB-INF/pages` location with the `.jsp` suffix, and all beans are configured under the `com.packt` package with Spring annotations.

4. Create a `LoginInfo` class in the `com.packt.model` package. This class represents the login information. Add two private string fields, `userId` and `password`, generate getters and setters

5. Create a JSP page called `login.jsp` under `/WEB-INF/pages` and add the following lines to create a form using the Spring tag library. Modify the form and add normal HTML input for username and password:

```
<%@ taglib prefix="sf" uri="http://www.springframework.org/tags/
form"%>
<sf:form method="POST" modelAttribute="loginInfo" action="/
onLogin">

</sf:form>
```

6. Create a controller class called com.packt.controller.LoginController to handle the login request. Add the following lines:

```
@Controller
@Scope("session")
public class LoginController implements Serializable {
  @RequestMapping({ "/", "/login" })
  public String onStartUp(ModelMap model) {
    model.addAttribute("loginInfo", new LoginInfo());
    return "login";
  }
}
```

The @Controller annotation indicates that the class is a Spring MVC controller class. In sample-servlet.xml, we defined <context:component-scan base-package="com.packt" />, so Spring will scan this @Controller annotation and create a bean. @RequestMapping maps any request with the default path /SpringMvcTest/ or /SpringMvcTest/login to the onStartUp method. This method returns a view named login. The view resolver defined in the XML file will map the login request to /WEB-INF/pages/login.jsp page.

7. Create another method in the Login class to handle the login submit request:

```
@RequestMapping({ "/onLogin" })
public String onLogin(@ModelAttribute("loginInfo")
    LoginInfo loginInfo, ModelMap model) {
  if(!"junit".equals(loginInfo.getUserId())) {
    model.addAttribute("error", "invalid login name");
    return "login";
      }
  if(!"password".equals(loginInfo.getPassword())) {
    model.addAttribute("error", "invalid password");
    return "login";
  }
    model.addAttribute("name", "junit reader!");
    return "greetings";
}
```

The method is mapped with /onLogin. @ModelAttribute("loginInfo") is the model submitted from the login.jsp form. This method checks whether the username is junit and password is password. If the user ID or password does not match, then an error message is shown in the login page; otherwise, the greetings view is opened.

8. Change `login.jsp` to submit the form to `/SpringMvcTest/onLogin`, and the `modelattribute` name is `loginInfo`:

```
<sf:form method="POST" modelAttribute="loginInfo" action="/
SpringMvcTest/onLogin">
```

Also, add the following JSTL expression to display the error message:

```
<h1>${error}</h1>
```

9. Create a JSP file called `greetings.jsp` and add the following lines:

```
<h1>Hello :${name}</h1>
```

10. In the browser, enter `http://localhost:8080/SpringMvcTest/`. This will open the `login` page. In the `login` page, do not enter any value; just hit **Submit**. It will show the error message **Invalid login name**. Now, enter `junit` in the `user Id` field and `password` in the `Password` field and hit *Enter*; the application will greet you with following message:

Resources: Spring Framework Reference Documentation

Summary

This chapter covered the Spring basics. It discussed the Spring projects and in particular Spring Framework. It explored the Spring container, Spring bean life cycle, dependency injection, AOP, Spring MVC, and Spring transaction management.

The next chapter will focus on getting the reader quickly started with JUnit 4 and the Mocking framework. It provides an overview of JUnit testing and explores the Mockito APIs.

2
Working with JUnit and Mockito

This chapter covers the unit testing concept, JUnit 4 framework, Eclipse setup, test doubles, and mocking with Mockito.

The following topics are covered in this chapter:

- JUnit 4 annotations
- Assertion methods and `assertThat`
- The `@RunWith` annotation
- Exception handling in JUnit
- JUnit test suite
- Overview of Mockito and Mockito APIs
- Advanced Mockito examples

Learning unit testing

A test is a measurement of performance of something, or an examination of data; for example, a class test is an assessment of our understanding, to determine whether we can go to the next level or not. We deliver software to our customers, so a test in the software context is the validation of a requirement before the software is delivered to a customer. For example, we need to check whether a valid user can log in to a system, or 1,000 concurrent users can access the system.

A unit test is a fundamental test to quickly assess whether the result of a computation can possibly go wrong or not. It is a straightforward check to verify the basis of the computation result.

Generally, Java code is unit tested using print statements or by debugging the application. Neither of these approaches is correct, and combining production code with testing logic is not good practice. Though it doesn't break the production code, it increases code complexity, degrades readability, and creates severe maintenance problems, or the production code may malfunction if anything gets misconfigured. When we add print statements or excessive logging statements in production code for unit testing, they get executed along with the production code and print needless information. In turn, they increase execution time and reduce code readability. Also, excessive logging might bury a genuine issue; for example, we might fail to notice a seriously hung thread message because of excessive logging.

Unit testing is the basis of **Test-Driven Development** (**TDD**). In TDD, a failing test is written first, then code is written to satisfy the test, and then the code quality is improved by refactoring the code and applying patterns. So unit tests drive the design. They reduce over engineering, as the code is written only to satisfy a failing test. Automated tests provide a quick regression safety net for refactoring and new features.

Kent Beck invented the **Extreme Programming** (**XP**) concept and TDD. He has authored many books and papers.

Generally, we don't mix production code with the test code, so unit tests are kept in the same project, but under a different directory or source folder such that the unit tests for an `org.packt.Bar.java` Java class should be written in an `org.packt.BarTest.java` test class. The convention is to end a test class name with `Test`. Note that the `Bar` class and `BarTest` have the same package (`org.packt`), but they should be organized in the `src` (`/org/foo/Bar.java`) and `test` (`/org/foo/BarTest.java`) source folders, respectively. Keeping the source code and the unit test code in the same package allows the unit test code to access the source code's protected and default methods and members. This approach is useful while working with the legacy code.

Generally, customers do not need the unit tests as they don't execute them, so during software packaging, the test folder is not bundled with the production code.

Code-driven unit testing frameworks are used to unit test Java code. The following are a few Java unit testing frameworks:

- SpryTest
- Jtest
- JUnit
- TestNG

The most popular and widely used framework is the JUnit framework. JUnit 4 will be explored in the following section.

Working with the JUnit framework

JUnit is the most popular unit testing framework for Java. It offers a metadata-based, non-invasive, and elegant unit testing framework for the Java community. Apparently, TestNG has cleaner syntax and usage than JUnit, but JUnit is far more popular than TestNG. JUnit enjoys better mocking support such as from Mockito, which offers a custom JUnit4 runner.

Version 4.12 is the latest JUnit framework version that can be downloaded from `https://github.com/junit-team/junit/wiki/Download-and-Install`.

JUnit 4 is a metadata-based (annotation), non-invasive (JUnit tests do not need to inherit from a framework class) framework. The JUnit framework provides APIs to write test cases to verify the individual functional flows, requirements, or units of code. JUnit evolved from an invasive framework to a non-invasive framework, so we must take a look at previous versions of JUnit framework to understand the benefits of JUnit 4. The following section compares the JUnit 4 framework with its predecessor. JUnit 3 had many downsides: it used to force your JUnit test to extend the `TestCase` class and override some methods, a test method had to start with `test`, and so on. The following are advantages of JUnit 4 over its predecessor:

- A test case no longer needs to inherit `junit.framework.Testcase`. Any POJO class can be a test class.

- To prepare and clean up test data in JUnit 3, the `setUp` and `tearDown` methods were used. You needed to override these methods explicitly, but with JUnit 4, you can annotate any method with the `@before` or `@after` annotations to execute it right before and after any test method, respectively.

- In JUnit 3, a test method name starts with `test <name...>`, but JUnit 4 allows you to annotate any public method with `@Test` to execute it as a test method.

Java **Integrated Development Environments (IDEs)** provide features such as step debugging, syntax highlighting, autocompletion, refactoring, and so on, and these features enable us to write and debug code more easily. Popular Java IDEs include Eclipse, NetBeans, JCreator, BlueJ, JBuilder, MyEclipse, IntelliJ IDEA, JDeveloper, and so on.

In this book, we'll use Eclipse for Java coding and JUnit testing. Eclipse can be downloaded from `http://www.eclipse.org/downloads/`.

The latest Eclipse IDE version is Luna (v4.4).

Eclipse releases a project annually. It started with a project named **Callisto** (starts with a C). Lexicographically, Eclipse project names go like C, E, G, H, I, J, K, and L.

Since 2006, they have released **Europa (E)**, **Ganymede (G)**, **Galileo (G)**, **Helios (H)**, **Indigo (I)**, **Juno (J)**, **Kepler (K)**, and **Luna (L)**.

The following section configures Eclipse and executes our first JUnit test.

Configuring Eclipse

This section can be skipped if you already know how to configure Eclipse and the classpath of the Java project. The following are the steps to configure Eclipse:

1. Go to the Eclipse download site, at http://www.eclipse.org/downloads/. To download the binary, choose an operating system from the drop-down (**Windows, Mac**, or **Linux**) and click on a hardware architecture hyperlink, that is, **32 Bit** or **64 Bit**. The following screenshot of Eclipse Kepler shows this. The latest version of Eclipse is Luna. For Spring users, it is better to install the Eclipse IDE for Java EE developers, which includes some Spring support and web development that will be used in the last chapter.

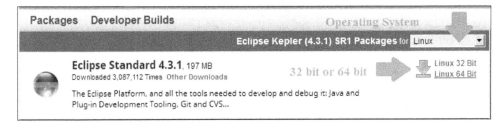

2. Unzip the Eclipse binary and click on eclipse.exe (in Windows) or run the ./Eclipse shell script (in Linux or Mac) to launch Eclipse.

3. Eclipse needs a workspace to manage project files. Enter a workspace name to create a new workspace; for example, in Windows, enter C:\myworkspace\junit, and in Linux or Mac, enter $HOME /workspace/junit. If the directories or folders don't exist, Eclipse will create the directory hierarchy for you and open the new workspace.

4. Now press *Ctrl + N* or click on the **New** menu option in **File**. A new wizard will pop up. In this wizard, select **Java Project** and click on **Next**. Enter the Java project name as `JUnitTests` and click on **Finish**. Eclipse will create the `JUnitTests` project.

5. In this chapter, we'll write JUnit tests, and for this, we need the JUnit framework JARs. To download the JUnit JARs, go to `https://github.com/junit-team/junit/wiki/Download-and-Install`, and download `junit.jar` and `hamcrest-core.jar`. Then copy the downloaded JARs to the `JUnitTests` project directory.

6. There are two ways to add the downloaded JUnit JARs to the project library or `classpath`. You can right-click on the downloaded JARs, select the **Build Path** menu, and then click on the **Add to build path** menu item; or you can right-click on the project, and when a pop-up menu appears, select the **Properties** menu item, click on **Java build path** on the left-hand side, and open the **Libraries** tab. In the **Libraries** tab, click on the **Add JARs...** button, it will pop up a projects window. Expand the **JUnitTests** project from the menu and select the two JARs (`junit.jar` and `hamcrest-core.jar`) to add them to **Libraries**. Now our **JUnitTests** project is ready for JUnit testing.

We read that JUnit 4 is a non-invasive, annotation-based framework and it doesn't ask us to extend any framework class. The following section uncovers JUnit 4 annotations, assertions, and exceptions.

We are going to examine annotations before writing our first test.

Examining annotations

The `@Test` annotation signifies a test. We can annotate any public method with `@Test` to make it a JUnit test method. We don't need to start a test method name with test.

To verify code logic, sometimes, we need to build data such that if a method accepts a list of students and publishes the result, the method internally sorts the student list based on the total marks obtained. Then, to unit test the sorting logic, we need to build a list of students and set individual totals. This activity of building the student list with marks is called **data setup**. JUnit 3 API provides a `setUp()` method in the `TestCase` class for data setup. A test class can override the `setUp()` method and write data population logic there. The following is the `setUp()` method signature:

```
protected void setUp() throws Exception
```

JUnit 4 doesn't define any method for data setup. Rather, it offers the `@Before` annotation. When a public void method of any name is annotated with `@Before`, then that method is executed prior to every test execution.

Similarly, when any public method is annotated with `@After`, the method gets executed subsequent to every test method execution. JUnit 3 defines a `tearDown()` method for this purpose.

JUnit 4 defines two method-level annotations, `@BeforeClass` and `@AfterClass`, for public static methods. Being static, they get executed only once per test class. Any public static method annotated with `@BeforeClass` gets executed prior to the first test, and any public static method annotated with `@AfterClass` gets executed following the last test.

The following example elucidates JUnit 4 annotations and the execution sequence of annotated methods:

1. Launch Eclipse and open the **JUnitTests** project. Create a source folder named `test`, and create a Java class named `SanityTest.java` under `com.packtpub.junit.recap` the package. The following screenshot explains this:

   The general convention to name test classes is that a test class name should end with a `Test` suffix such that a `SomeClass` class will have a `SomeClassTest` test class. Several code coverage tools ignore the tests if the test classes don't end with a `Test` suffix.

2. We have created the test class. Now add the following code snippet to the `SanityTest` class:

   ```
   import org.junit.After;
   import org.junit.AfterClass;
   import org.junit.Before;
   import org.junit.BeforeClass;
   import org.junit.Test;
   ```

```java
public class SanityTest {

  @BeforeClass
  public static void beforeClass() {
    System.out.println("***Before Class is invoked");
  }

  @Before
  public void before() {
    System.out.println("_____");
    System.out.println("\t Before is invoked");
  }
  @After
  public void after() {
    System.out.println("\t After is invoked");
    System.out.println("=================");
  }

  @Test
  public void someTest() {
    System.out.println("\t\t someTest is invoked");
  }

  @Test
  public void someTest2() {
    System.out.println("\t\t someTest2 is invoked");
  }


  @AfterClass
  public static void afterClass() {
    System.out.println("***After Class is invoked");
  }
}
```

The SanityTest class defines six methods. Two methods are annotated with the @Test, two public static methods are annotated with the @BeforeClass and @AfterClass annotations, and the other two non-static methods are annotated with the @Before and @After annotations.

The static method annotated with @BeforeClass gets executed only once—before the SanityTest class is instantiated (in other words, before the first test method execution), and the method annotated with @AfterClass gets executed after both the test methods have finished executing.

3. We'll run the tests to understand the method execution sequence. To run the tests, press *Alt + Shift + X + T* or navigate to **Run | Run As | JUnit Test**. During test execution, the following console (System.out.println) output will be displayed:

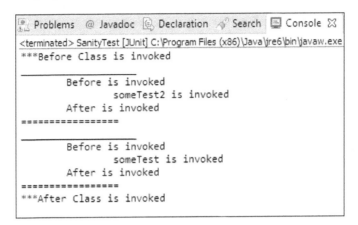

```
  Problems   @ Javadoc   Declaration   Search   Console
<terminated> SanityTest [JUnit] C:\Program Files (x86)\Java\jre6\bin\javaw.exe
***Before Class is invoked
_____
        Before is invoked
              someTest2 is invoked
        After is invoked
==================
_____
        Before is invoked
              someTest is invoked
        After is invoked
==================
***After Class is invoked
```

Ensure that the `before` and `after` methods are executed before and after every test method execution, respectively. However, the order of test method execution varies from environment to environment, so `someTest` may get executed before `someTest2` in your machine, or vice versa. The `afterClass` and `beforeClass` methods are executed only once.

Congratulations! You have executed your first JUnit 4 test and learned the annotations.

> The `@Before` and `@After` annotations can be applied to any public void method. The `@AfterClass` and `@BeforeClass` annotations can be applied only to public static void methods.

Verifying an expectation with an assertion

An assertion verifies a programming hypothesis with the actual result of a code execution. For example, you can expect that when you add a set of positive numbers, the addition will result in a positive number. So you can write an `add` method to add a set of numbers and assert the expected result with the actual result. For example, you can pass 1, 2, and 3 to the `add` method and expect that the result will be 6, so you can assert 6 with the actual result of the program. If the outcome doesn't match the expectation, the assertion fails, which implies that there must be some problem in your coding logic. Therefore, you need to revisit the logic.

The `org.junit.Assert` class offers a set of static overloaded methods to assert expected and real values for all primitive types, objects, and arrays.

Note that all assert methods have a version with a string message as the first argument, and the string message is shown if the assertion fails. The following are the handy assert methods:

- `assertTrue(assert condition)` or `assertTrue(failure message, assert condition)`: If the assert condition becomes `false`, the assertion fails and the `assertTrue` method throws an `AssertionError`. When a failure message is passed, the failure message is thrown.

- `assertFalse(boolean condition)` or `assertFalse(failure message, boolean condition)`: These assert methods expect that the Boolean condition passed to the method will be `false`; for example, if we expect that user login will not be successful and call `isValidUser()`, or expect that an object will be `null` and check `obj == null`, but if the condition becomes `true`, such that the `isValidUser()` method returns `true` or `obj` does not become `null`, then the assertion fails and the `assertFalse` method throws an `AssertionError` with the passed-in error message.

- `assertNull`: This method expects that the passed in argument will be `null`. If the argument does not become `null`, the assertion fails and the method throws an `AssertionError`. This is useful when we pass invalid inputs to a method and expect that the output will be `null`.

- `assertNotNull`: This method expects that the passed-in argument will not be `null`. If the argument becomes `null`, the assertion fails and the method throws an `AssertionError`. Suppose you are invoking a method and getting a response object. You can assert the response for not null and then check other attributes of the response.

- `assertEquals(string message, object expected, object actual)` or `assertEquals(object expected, object actual)` or `assertEquals(primitive expected, primitive actual)`: This method takes two arguments, the expected value and the actual value, and compares their values. If the arguments don't match, it raises an `AssertionError`. When primitive values are passed to this method, the values are compared. If objects are passed, the `equals()` method is invoked such that `expected` equals `actual`.

- `assertSame(object expected, object actual)`: This method expects that two same object references will be passed to the method. It checks the object reference using the `==` operator and throws an `AssertionError` if two different objects are passed.

- `assertNotSame`: This method expects that two different object references will be passed to the method. The assertion fails if the same object references are passed.

> At times, `double` value computation leads to unexpected results due to the representation that Java uses to store double values. The following example demonstrates the uncertainty in double value computation.
>
> Declare a `double` variable, `result = .999 + .98`. The result variable should hold the `1.98` value, but if you print the result to the console, the output displayed is `1.9889999999999999`. So, if you assert the result with a double value of `1.98`, the assertion will fail.
>
> Due to this uncertainty in double computation, the `Assert` class doesn't rely on double comparison, hence the `assertEquals(double expected, double actual)` method has been deprecated.
>
> Alternatively, `Assert` offers an overloaded `assertEquals` method for double value assertion, which is `assertEquals(double expected, double actual, double delta)`. The third argument, `delta`, is very important during double value comparison when the `expected` value doesn't match the `actual` value because if the difference between them is less than or equal to the `delta` value, the assertion is considered to be passed.
>
> For monetary calculations, never use double values; instead, use `BigDecimal`.

We'll examine the `assert` methods in the following example:

1. Add a JUnit test class named `AssertTest` to the `com.packtpub.junit.recap` package, and include the following code snippet in this class:

```java
package com.packtpub.junit.recap;

import org.junit.Assert;
import org.junit.Test;

public class AssertTest {

  @Test
  public void assert_boolean_conditions() throws Exception
  {
    Assert.assertTrue(true);
    Assert.assertFalse(false);
  }
```

```
@Test
public void assert_null_and_not_null_object_values()
throws Exception {
  Object object = null;
  Assert.assertNull(object);

  object = new String("String value");
  Assert.assertNotNull(object);
  }
}
```

The assert_boolean_conditions test sends true to assertTrue and false to assertFalse. If you pass false to assertTrue or true to assertFalse, the test will fail.

The assert_null_and_not_null_object_values test creates a null object, passes it to the assertNull method, reassigns a string value to the object, and passes the string to the assertNotNull.

Now run the tests. They should be green.

2. Now we'll inspect the behavior of assertEquals. Include the following test snippet in the class. In the preceding example, we used the assert method in a static way. Now we will static import the assertEquals method and invoke the assert methods like a local method:

```
import static org.junit.Assert.assertEquals;

@Test
public void assert_equals_test() throws Exception {
    Integer anInteger = 5;
    Integer anotherInteger = 5;
    assertEquals(anInteger, anotherInteger);
}
```

This test initializes two integer objects, anInteger and anotherInteger, with value equal to 5, and passes them to the assertEquals method. In turn, the assertEquals method calls anInteger.equals(anotherInteger). Since the values are the same, the equals method returns true, and the assertion passes. Note that the assertEquals method compares the values, and assertSame compares the references.

If you want to assert double values, either use the delta version of assertEquals(actual, expected, delta), or try using BigDecimal instead of double values.

3. We'll validate the behavior of `assertNotSame`, add the following test to the test class, and static-import the assert method:

```
import static org.junit.Assert.assertNotSame;

@Test
public void assert_not_same_test() throws Exception {
    Integer anInt = new Integer("5");
    Integer anotherInt = new Integer("5");
    assertNotSame(anInt , anotherInt);
}
```

The `assertNotSame` method raises `AssertionError` when the expected object reference and the actual object reference point to the same memory location. Here, `anInt` and `anotherInt` hold the same value, but they point to two different memory locations. Hence the `assertNotSame` method passes.

4. Now we'll inspect the behavior of `assertSame`. Add the following test to the test class and static-import the assert method:

```
import static org.junit.Assert.assertSame;

@Test
public void assert_same_test() throws Exception {
    Integer anInt = new Integer("5");
    Integer anotherInt = anInt;
    assertSame(anInt, anotherInt);
}
```

Here, the test passes because `anInt` and `anotherInt` have the same memory reference.

Examining exception handling

This section deals with exceptions in JUnit tests. In a JUnit test, when a test method throws an exception, the test fails, and the test method marks the test as erroneous. We should be allowed to unit test the exceptional condition such that an API takes two objects and throws an exception if any argument is passed as `null`. If we pass a `null` value to the API, the test fails with an error, but actually, an exception is not an error. Rather, it is desirable, and the test should fail if the API doesn't throw an exception.

JUnit 4 provides a mechanism to handle the preceding situation.

The `@Test` annotation takes an `expected=<<Exception class name>>.class` argument.

When we annotate a test method with `@Test` and pass an expected exception to the annotation, but during execution, the expected exception doesn't match the real exception thrown from the test method or the test method doesn't throw an exception, the test fails. The following test snippet examines exception handling:

```
@Test(expected=RuntimeException.class)
public void test_exception_condition() {
    throw new RuntimeException();
}
```

This exception handling mechanism doesn't allow you to verify the error message. JUnit 4 provides several other mechanisms that are usually considered to be better solutions, such as `@Rule`, an `ExpectedException` rule that lets you examine the message as well as the type.

Working with the @RunWith annotation

Test runners perform JUnit test execution. When we run JUnit tests in Eclipse, we get a graphical output such as a green bar or red bar. Eclipse has a native, built-in graphical runner for executing the JUnit tests.

The `@RunWith` annotation accepts a class name. The class should extend the `org.junit.runner.Runner` class. An example of a runner is `JUnit4.class`. This class is also known as the default JUnit 4 class runner.

When we annotate a test class with `@RunWith` or extend a `@RunWith` class, during test execution, the built-in JUnit4 runner is ignored. Instead, JUnit uses the runner that it references in the `@RunWith` argument.

A runner can change the characteristics of the test class; for example, a Spring runner enables Spring context initialization nature, or a Mockito runner initializes proxy objects annotated with the `@Mock` annotation.

`Suite` is a standard runner that allows us to build a suite that contains tests from many packages. The following is an example of `@RunWith`:

```
@RunWith(Suite.class)
public class MySuite {

}
```

Working with test suites

A test suite groups and executes multiple tests. From Eclipse, we can run individual test classes, but to run multiple tests together, we need a test suite. To achieve this, JUnit 4 offers the `Suite.class` class and the `@Suite.SuiteClasses` annotation. This annotation accepts a comma-separated array of test classes.

Add a Java class named `TestSuite` and annotate it with `@RunWith(Suite.class)`. As a result, the suite runner will be responsible for executing the test class.

Annotate the `TestSuite` class with `@Suite.SuiteClasses` and pass a comma-separated array of other test classes, such as (`{ AssertTest.class, TestExecutionOrder.class, Assumption.class }`).

The following is the code snippet for the test suites:

```
import org.junit.runner.RunWith;
import org.junit.runners.Suite;

@RunWith(Suite.class)
@Suite.SuiteClasses({ AssertTest.class, TestExecutionOrder.class,
    Assumption.class })
public class TestSuite {

}
```

When we execute the `TestSuite` class, it in turn executes all the test classes passed to the `@Suite.SuiteClasses` annotation. The following screenshot demonstrates the result of test suite execution:

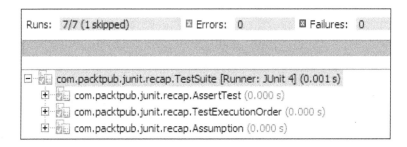

Working with assertThat

The assertThat method was added to the Assert class to verify a result in a sophisticated way. Joe Walnes invented the assertThat(Object actual, Matcher matcher) method. The assertThat method is comprehensible and easier to use than the assertEquals method.

The following is the assertThat syntax:

```
public static void assertThat(Object actual, Matcher matcher)
```

Object represents the value received, and Matcher is an implementation of the org. hamcrest.Matcher interface. The Matcher interface is not a part of the JUnit jar. Rather, the interface is defined in a separate library called hamcrest.jar.

The assertEquals method compares the expected value with the actual value, and fails if the values do not match, whereas with a matcher, the assertThat method may either compare the object partially with the matcher or may look for an exact match. The Matcher interface offers an array of utility methods such as is, either, or, not, and hasItem for partial and exact matches. The Matcher methods follow the builder pattern to create a chain of commands. It can combine one or more matchers to build a composite matcher chain. This behavior is similar to the StringBuilder method, which builds a target string in numerous steps.

The following examples demonstrate the capabilities of Matcher and assertThat:

- assertThat(calculatedTax, is(not(thirtyPercent)));
- assertThat(phdStudentList, hasItem(DrJohn));
- assertThat(manchesterUnitedClub, both(is(EPL_Champion)). and(is(UEFA_Champions_League_Champion)));

Honestly speaking, the examples are more readable as English statements than pieces of mundane JUnit test code. Anyone who understands English can understand the objective of the test. This way, a matcher can improve the readability of your tests.

Hamcrest offers a utility matcher class, org.hamcrest.CoreMatchers, with an array of utility matcher methods. A few utility methods of CoreMatchers are allOf, anyOf, both, either, describedAs, everyItem, is, isA, anything, hasItem, hasItems, equalTo, any, instanceOf, not, nullValue, notNullValue, sameInstance, theInstance ,startsWith, endsWith, and containsString. These methods return a Matcher to build a chain of commands.

In the preceding section, we used the assertEquals method. The following section will start with the equalTo method, which is similar to the assertEquals method.

Exploring equalTo, is, and not

Add a JUnit test class named `AssertThatTest.java`, and static-import the utility methods of `CoreMatchers`. The following is the test code snippet for the `equalTo`, `is` and `not` matchers:

```java
import static org.hamcrest.CoreMatchers.*;
import static org.junit.Assert.assertThat;

import org.junit.Test;

public class AssertThatTest {

  @Test
  public void test_matcher_behavior() throws Exception {
    int myAge = 30;

    //examine the exact match with equalTo and is
    assertThat(myAge, equalTo(30));
    assertThat(myAge, is(30));

   //examine partial match with not()
    assertThat(myAge, not(equalTo(33)));
    assertThat(myAge, is(not(33)));
  }
}
```

The `equalTo` method behaves like the `==` operator. We initialized the `myAge` variable to `30`, and then passed it to the `assertThat` method with an `equalTo(30)` matcher. The `equalTo` method accepts a value. If the `Matcher` value matches the expected value, the assertion passes. Otherwise, the `assertThat` method throws an `AssertionError`.

When we initialize `myAge` to `29` and rerun the test, the matcher value, `30`, doesn't match with `29`, so the assertion fails. The following screenshot demonstrates the resulting error message:

```
java.lang.AssertionError:
    Expected: <30>
       but: was <29>
  at org.hamcrest.MatcherAssert.assertThat(MatcherAssert.java:20)
```

The `is(value)` method accepts a value or matcher; it works similar to `equalTo(value)`. We can combine utility methods in it; for example, `is(value)` can be combined with `equalTo(value)` to build `is(equalTo(a))`, which is similar to `is(value)` or `equalTo(value)`.

The not method accepts a value or a matcher. The preceding test calls
assertThat(age, is(not(33)));. This expression can be translated as age is
not 33. So again, we can see that a Matcher expression is more comprehensible
than the assert methods.

Exploring compound matchers – either, both, anyOf, and allOf

This section explores the either, both, anyOf, and allOf compound matcher methods
in conjunction with not. Include the following test method in AssertThatTest.java:

```
@Test
  public void verify_multiple_values() throws Exception {

    double myMarks = 100.00;
    assertThat(myMarks, either(is(100.00)).or(is(90.9)));

    assertThat(myMarks, both(not(99.99)).and(not(60.00)));

    assertThat(myMarks, anyOf(is(100.00),is(1.00),is(55.00),
      is(88.00),is(67.8)));

    assertThat(myMarks, not(anyOf(is(0.00),is(200.00))));

    assertThat(myMarks, not(allOf(is(1.00),is(100.00),
      is(30.00))));
  }
```

The myMarks variable is initialized to 100.00. Then the value is asserted with an
either matcher. The either matcher method is used to compare two values against
a computed value in conjunction with the or matcher. If none of these two values
match with the computed value, an AssertionError is thrown.

The following is the syntax of the either(Matcher) method. It takes a matcher
and returns a CombinableEitherMatcher class. This class defines an or(Matcher
other) method to combine with the either Matcher method.

The or(Matcher other) method is translated as return (new
CombinableMatcher(first)).or(second);, and finally to new
CombinableMatcher(new AnyOf(templatedListWith(second)));.

The `both` method returns `true` only if the two values passed to it match the computed value. Otherwise, an `AssertionError` is thrown. The `both` method is used in conjunction with the `and` method to match the two values.

A numeric value, such as `myMarks`, cannot be equal to both `60` and `80`. We can, however, negate the expression and check that `myMarks` is not equal to `80` and `60`, using the `both` matcher as `assertThat(myMarks, both (not(60)). and(not (80)))`.

The `anyOf` matcher method is more like the `either` method with multiple values. The `anyOf` method compares multiple values against a computed value. If any of these values matches the computed value, the assertion is passed. If none of these values match the computed value, an `AssertionError` is thrown.

The `allOf` matcher method is more like the `both` matcher method with multiple values. The `allOf` method compares multiple values against a computed value. If any of these values does not match with the computed value, an `AssertionError` is thrown. Like the `both` method, we can combine `allOf` with `not` to ensure that a computed value either belongs to a set or does not belong to it.

In the preceding test, we combined `allOf` with `not` to check that `myMarks` is not `1`, `100`, or `30`.

Exploring collection matchers – hasItem and hasItems

In the preceding example, we asserted a single value against a set of values. This section asserts a collection of values against a value or a set of values.

Suppose you have a service API that returns you a list of salaries in your company, and you need to verify that the salaries include a particular amount or the CEO's salary. We'll mock the service API, create a salary list, and populate the list with the following values: `50.00`, `200.00`, and `500.00`. Suppose we would like to find whether a particular salary is included to the salary list or not. The `Matcher` API provides the `hasItem` method to check whether a value is included in a collection, and the `hasItems` method is used to check whether multiple values are included in a collection. The following code snippet demonstrates the capabilities of `hasItem` and `hasItems`:

```
@Test
public void verify_collection_values() throws Exception {

    List<Double> salary =Arrays.asList(50.0, 200.0, 500.0);
```

```
        assertThat(salary, hasItem(50.00));
        assertThat(salary, hasItems(50.00, 200.00));
            assertThat(salary, not(hasItem(1.00)));
    }
```

The `hasItem` method has two variants — one accepts a value and the other accepts a matcher. To check whether a particular value belongs to a collection, we can combine the `hasItem` method with `not`. The `hasItems` matcher works on a set of values.

Working with string matchers – startsWith, endsWith, and containsString

This section explores string matchers. The `CoreMatchers` class has three built-in matcher methods (`startsWith`, `endsWith`, and `containsString`) to work with the strings. The following code assigns a value to the `myName` string variable, asserts that `myName` starts with a particular value and contains a particular value, and checks whether `myName` ends with a particular value:

```
@Test
  public void verify_Strings() throws Exception {
      String myName = "John Jr Dale";
      assertThat(myName, startsWith("John"));
      assertThat(myName, endsWith("Dale"));
      assertThat(myName, containsString("Jr"));
  }
```

The `startsWith` method verifies that the passed string starts with a given string, the `endsWith` method checks whether the passed-in string ends with a given string, and the `containsString` verifies that the passed-in string contains a particular string.

 Strings are objects, so we can use built-in matchers such as `both`, `either`, `anyOf`, and so on with string objects to verify string values.

Exploring custom matchers

So far we have used built-in framework matchers with the `assertThat` method. This section covers a custom matcher that will work with the `assertThat` method. We'll be building this matcher to compare two values and return `true` only if the actual object is less than or equal to the expected value. We'll name it the `lessThanOrEqual` matcher. It will operate on any `Comparable` objects such as objects of `Integer`, `Double`, or `String` types, and any object that implements the `Comparable` interface.

The following examples explain the behavior of the custom matcher. You will see that assertThat(10, lessThanOrEqual(11)) will pass but assertThat(10, lessThanOrEqual(5)) will fail, and assertThat("john100", lessThanOrEqual("john100")) will pass but assertThat("john123", lessThanOrEqual("john12")) will fail.

The following are the steps to be performed to build the lessThanOrEqual matcher:

1. Add a Java class named LessThanOrEqual under the com.packtpub.junit. recap package.

2. All matchers implement the Matcher interface, though Hamcrest recommends extending the org.hamcrest.BaseMatcher class instead of implementing the Matcher interface. Therefore, we'll follow the convention and extend BaseMatcher. The abstract BaseMatcher class implements the Matcher interface, but it doesn't implement the describeTo(Description description) and matches(Object t) methods. The class that extends the BaseMatcher class should provide the implementation of the abstract describeTo and matches methods .

    Internally, the assertThat method invokes the matches(Object obj) method. An AssertionError is thrown if the matches method returns false, and the describeTo(Description description) method is called to build the error description.

    The following code fragment shows the internals of the assertThat method:

    ```
    if(!matcher.matches(actual)){
            Description description = new StringDescription();

            description.appendText(reason).appendText
            ("\nExpected: ").appendDescriptionOf(matcher).
            appendText("\n    but: ");

            matcher.describeMismatch(actual, description);
            throw new AssertionError(description.toString());
    }
    ```

    When the matcher.matches() method returns false, a description object is created and the error description is populated. The appendDescriptionOf() method invokes the describeTo() method of the matcher and builds the error description.

    The matcher.describeMismatch(actual, description) method call appends the was <<actual>> string to the description, where <<actual>> represents the actual value, which doesn't match the expected value.

3. The `lessThanOrEqual` class compares two objects to determine whether one object is less than or equal to the other object so that the matcher can operate on the `Comparable` objects. Our matcher should work on any object type that can be compared, so the generic matcher will operate on any type, `T`, that implements the `Comparable` interface. The following is our matcher definition:

```
public class LessThanOrEqual<T extends Comparable<T>>
    extends BaseMatcher<Comparable<T>> {

}
```

4. Our matcher extends the `BaseMatcher` class, so it has to implement the `describeTo()` and `matches()` superclass methods. The `assertThat` method invokes the `matches(Object o)` method of the matcher with the actual value. When we pass an expected value to the matcher, during assertion, the `assertThat` method calls the `matches` method of the matcher with the actual value, and the matcher compares the actual value with the expected value.

The following code snippet explains the `assertThat` call:

```
assertThat (actual, matcher(expectedValue)).
```

We need to store the `expectedValue` during the `Matcher(LessThanOrEqual)` object instantiation, and compare it with the actual value in the `matches()` method. The following is our matcher class:

```
public class LessThanOrEqual<T extends Comparable<T>> extends
BaseMatcher<Comparable<T>> {
   private final Comparable<T> expValue;

   public LessThanOrEqual(T expValue) {
       this.expValue= expValue;
   }

   @Override
   public void describeTo(Description desc) {
       desc.appendText(" less than or equal(<=)"
         +expValue);
   }

   @Override
   public boolean matches(Object t) {
     int compareTo = expValue.compareTo((T)t);
     return compareTo > -1;
   }
}
```

The `matches` method of the `LessThanOrEqual` class should return `true` only if `expValue.compareTo(actual) >= 0` is true, but when the expected value is less than the actual value, then the `matches` method returns `false`, the assertion fails, and `describeTo` appends the `"less than or equals (<=)
" + expValue` string to the error message.

5. The `assertThat` method accepts a matcher, so we can pass `new LessThanOrEqual(expectedValue)` to the `assertThat` method, but the camel case class name reduces readability. Instead, a method name starting with a small letter could improve readability.

   Add a static method named `lessThanOrEqual()` to the `LessThanOrEqual` class, and instantiate a new object of `LessThanOrEqual`. Pass the `lessThanOrEqual()` method to the `assertThat` method. The following is the code snippet for the custom matcher:

```
@Factory
public static<T extends Comparable<T>>  Matcher<T>
   lessThanOrEqual(T t) {
       return new LessThanOrEqual(t);
}
```

6. To validate the `LessThanOrEqual` matcher, you have to static-import the `LessThanOrEqual` class and add a test to the `AssertThatTest` class. The following test method passes integer, double, and string values to the matcher. The test passes because the actual value is always less than or equal to the expected value:

```
@Test
public void lessthanOrEquals_ matcher() throws
   Exception
{
   int actualGoalScored = 2;
  int expGoalScored= 4;
   assertThat(actualGoalScored,
       lessThanOrEqual(expGoalScored));
   expGoalScored =2;
   assertThat(actualGoalScored,
       lessThanOrEqual(expGoalScored ));

   double actualDouble = 3.14;
   double expDouble = 9.00;
   assertThat(actualDouble, lessThanOrEqual(expDouble));
```

```
        String authorName = "Sujoy";
        String expAuthName = "Zachary";
        assertThat(authorName, lessThanOrEqual(expAuthName));
    }
```

7. Now we'll test the opposite scenario—where the actual value is greater than the expected value. In Java, `Integer.MAX_VALUE` represents the maximum integer value and `Integer.MIN_VALUE` represents the minimum integer value. If we imagine that the maximum value would be less than or equal to the minimum value, then the assertion will fail. The following code snippet shows this comparison:

```
    int maxInt = Integer.MAX_VALUE;
    assertThat(maxInt, lessThanOrEqual(Integer.MIN_VALUE));
```

As the `MAX_VALUE` is not less than the `MIN_VALUE`, the assertion fails and gives this error:

```
java.lang.AssertionError:
    Expected: less than or equals(<=) -2147483648
        but: was <2147483647>
    at org.hamcrest.MatcherAssert.assertThat(MatcherAssert.java:20)
    at org.junit.Assert.assertThat(Assert.java:865)
```

Working with Mockito

Mockito is an open source unit mocking framework for Java. It allows mock object creation, verification, and stubbing.

Mockito was moved to GitHub. You can visit `https://github.com/mockito/mockito` to get the source code, and visit `http://code.google.com/p/mockito/` to learn more about Mockito.

Learning the significance of Mockito

We add automated unit tests to run and notify us in case any code breaks the system so that the wrong code can be identified and fixed very quickly.

But when an automated test suite takes time to execute, for instance, two hours to complete a build, it defeats the purpose of quick feedback. In **Test-Driven Development (TDD)**, automated JUnit test cases are run to provide quick feedback. Here, a test should not take more than a few milliseconds to execute. When a test suite takes hours to execute, it blocks the progress of development.

A test suite takes time because individual tests take time to execute. The following are some reasons behind delays in test execution:

- A test performs an integration task, such as acquiring a database connection, and then fetches data or updates data.

- A test may connect to the Internet to download files or get the current stock price.

- A test may send an invoice mail to a vendor. In order to send an e-mail, it has to interact with an SMTP server.

- A test may print a bill, open a file, or perform an I/O operation.

Do we really need to perform all or any of these tasks to unit test our code?

If we don't perform these tasks, a few parts of the system remain untested. So querying the database or sending an e-mail is necessary to perform end-to-end system testing, but when a test interacts with an external resource, it is called an integration test. Due to external resource interaction, integration tests take time to execute but unit tests mock external dependencies using test doubles, and thus unit tests are executed very quickly.

Mockito provides APIs to mock external dependencies. It can mock a database connection with a mock implementation that doesn't interact with the real database, or it can mock an SMTP connection for an e-mail task. So Mockito provides APIs to isolate the actual logic from external dependencies to unit test it.

Exploring Mockito

We need to download the Mockito binary to start working with Mockito. You can download the Mockito jar from `http://mockito.org/`.

As of December 2014, the latest Mockito version is v2.0.2-beta.

The following section configures Eclipse projects to use Mockito.

Configuring Mockito

To add Mockito JAR files as a project dependency, perform the following steps:

1. Unzip the Mockito JAR files into a folder.

2. Open Eclipse.

3. In Eclipse, create a Java project named `MockitoOverview`.

4. Right-click on the project. A pop-up menu will appear. Expand the **Build Path** menu and click on the **Configure Build Path** menu item. It will open a wizard. Go to the **Libraries** tab in the Java build path.

5. Click on the **Add External JARs...** button and browse to the **Mockito** folder.

6. Select all JAR files and click on **OK**.

Mocking in action

This section provides examples of mock objects with a stock quote simulation program. The program observes the market trend and performs the following actions:

- Buying new stocks
- Selling existing stocks

The important domain objects in this program are Stock, MarketWatcher, Portfolio, and StockBroker.

The Stock class represents real-world stocks. A Stock object can have properties such as symbol, company name, and price.

The MarketWatcher object observes the market trend and returns the current stock price. A real-world MarketWatcher object needs to connect to the Internet to download the stock quote.

The Portfolio object represents a stock portfolio such stock count and price details. It provides APIs to get the average stock price and methods to buy and sell stocks. Suppose you bought a Facebook share for $75, and the next day, you bought one more Facebook share for $85. So, on the second day, you have two Facebook shares, with the average share price equal to $80.

Here is a screenshot of the Eclipse project. This project can be downloaded from the Packt Publishing website.

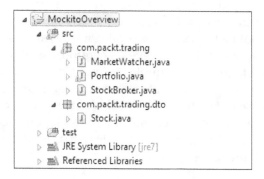

The following is the `StockBroker` class. It works together with the `MarketWatcher` and `Portfolio` classes. The `perform()` method accepts a portfolio and a stock, gets the current market price of the stock, and compares the current price with the average stock price. If the current stock price goes up 10 percent, then it sells 10 stocks. Otherwise, it buys a stock:

```java
public class StockBroker {
   private final static BigDecimal LIMIT
               = new BigDecimal("0.10");

   private final MarketWatcher market;

   public StockBroker(MarketWatcher market) {
      this.market = market;
   }

   public void perform(Portfolio portfolio,Stock stock) {
      Stock liveStock = market.getQuote(stock.getSymbol());
      BigDecimal avgPrice = portfolio.getAvgPrice(stock);
      BigDecimal priceGained =
            liveStock.getPrice().subtract(avgPrice);
      BigDecimal percentGain = priceGained.divide(avgPrice);
      if(percentGain.compareTo(LIMIT) > 0) {
         portfolio.sell(stock, 10);
      }else if(percentGain.compareTo(LIMIT) < 0){
         portfolio.buy(stock);
      }
   }
}
```

The `Portfolio` class reads the average stock price from the database, and the `MarketWatcher` class connects to the Internet to get the latest stock price. Therefore, if we need to write a unit test for the broker program, the test will need a database and an Internet connection. The test will interact with external entities, and we can call it an integration test rather than a unit test. If our unit tests interact with the real database and Internet connection, then chances of test failure will increase, as the database state might not be the same across all test runs, and each Internet call to get the stock price might return different values. Therefore asserting a constant value may result in assertion failure; for example, we assert a stock price of $100 in our test but the actual market price goes down to $90, or our test thinks that a portfolio has 10 stocks in the database but some other user adds 20 more shares using a different thread. That's why unit tests mock external dependencies and set a constant value as the expectation, so the preceding example will lead to this: all the time, the portfolio will return 10 as the number of stocks, or the current stock price will always be returned as $100.

In the following section, we'll mock external dependencies using Mockito and execute the test in isolation. Therefore, the test will invoke methods on proxy dependency objects and be self-governing, and thus it will be executed quickly.

Mocking objects

The `org.mockito.Mockito` class defines a static method `mock()` to create mock objects. The following code snippet creates mock objects using the `mock` method:

```java
import org.mockito.Mockito;

public class StockBrokerTest {
  MarketWatcher marketWatcher =
                  Mockito.mock(MarketWatcher.class);
  Portfolio portfolio =
                  Mockito.mock(Portfolio.class);

}
```

Instead of directly calling the `Mockito.mock()` method, we can use the static import feature of Java. The following code snippet simplifies mock creation using static import:

```java
import static org.mockito.Mockito.mock;

public class StockBrokerTest {
  MarketWatcher marketWatcher = mock(MarketWatcher.class);
  Portfolio portfolio = mock(Portfolio.class);
}
```

The alternative is to annotate the class member variables with the `@Mock` annotation. The following code snippet uses this annotation:

```java
import org.mockito.Mock;

public class StockBrokerTest {
  @Mock
  MarketWatcher marketWatcher;
  @Mock
  Portfolio portfolio;
}
```

To create mocks using the `@Mock` annotation, we need to initialize the mocks before test execution, so use `MockitoAnnotations.initMocks(this)` before using the mocks, or use `MockitoJUnitRunner` as a JUnit runner.

This example uses MockitoAnnotations:

```
import static org.junit.Assert.assertEquals;
import org.mockito.MockitoAnnotations;

public class StockBrokerTest {

  @Mock
  MarketWatcher marketWatcher;

  @Mock
  Portfolio portfolio;

  @Before
  public void setUp() {
    MockitoAnnotations.initMocks(this);
  }


  @Test
  public void sanity() throws Exception {
    assertNotNull(marketWatcher);
    assertNotNull(portfolio);
  }
}
```

The following example uses the MockitoJUnitRunner JUnit runner:

```
import org.mockito.runners.MockitoJUnitRunner;

@RunWith(MockitoJUnitRunner.class)
public class StockBrokerTest {

  @Mock
    MarketWatcher marketWatcher;

  @Mock
    Portfolio portfolio;

  @Test
    public void sanity() throws Exception {
      assertNotNull(marketWatcher);
      assertNotNull(portfolio);
  }
}
```

A few things to remember

Mockito cannot mock or spy on Java constructs such as final classes and methods, static methods, enums, private methods, the equals() and hashCode() methods, primitive types, and anonymous classes.

But the good news is that PowerMockito (an extension of the Mockito framework) API allows us to overcome the limitations of Mockito. It lets us mock static and private methods. You can also set expectations on new invocations for local or anonymous classes, private member classes, and inner classes but as per the design, you should not opt for mocking private or static properties because it violates the encapsulation. Instead, you should refactor the offending code to make it testable.

Now, to cross-check the information of a final class that Mockito cannot mock, just modify the Portfolio class and make it a final class. Then rerun the test. It will fail because the class is final.

The following screenshot shows the output of the JUnit test run:

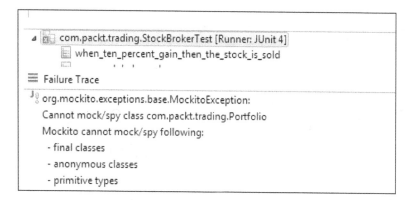

Stubbing methods

Stubbing a method means setting up an expectation on a method invocation or simulating the behavior of the method. Mock objects are basically proxy objects, and they imitate the behavior of real objects. We can stub a method on a mock object to redefine the behavior of the method. In other words, we can return a specific value or throw a specific exception when the method is called on the mocked object. If we don't stub a method of a mock object, the mock object returns the default values such as false for the Boolean return type, null for the object return type, 0 for the integer or long return type, and so on.

Mockito allows stubbing to return a specific value when a specific method is called. The `Mockito.when()` method identifies a method that needs to be stubbed, and the `thenReturn()` method returns a specific value.

The `when` static method is defined in the Mockito class. Here is the process of importing the `when` method in our test class:

```
import static org.mockito.Mockito.when;
```

The following example stubs the `getQuote(String symbol)` method of `MarketWatcher` and returns a specific `Stock` object:

```
import static org.mockito.Matchers.anyString;
import static org.mockito.Mockito.when;

@RunWith(MockitoJUnitRunner.class)
public class StockBrokerTest {

    @Mock MarketWatcher marketWatcher;
    @Mock Portfolio portfolio;

    @Test
    public void marketWatcher_Returns_current_stock_status() {
        Stock uvsityCorp = new Stock("UV", "Uvsity Corporation",
            new BigDecimal("100.00"));

        when(marketWatcher.getQuote(anyString())).
                thenReturn(uvsityCorp);

        assertNotNull(marketWatcher.getQuote("UV"));
    }
```

The preceding test method creates a stock object and stubs the `getQuote` method of `marketWatcher` to return the stock. Note that we passed `anyString()` to the `getQuote` method, and `anyString` represents any string value such as `"UV"`, which we passed in the next line (`marketWatcher.getQuote("UV")`). Therefore, whenever the `getQuote` method will be called on the `marketWatcher` proxy, the stock object will be returned.

The `when()` method represents the trigger for the time to stub.

The following Mockito methods represent the course of action of the trigger:

- `thenReturn(value to be returned)`: This returns a specific value.

- `thenThrow(throwable to be thrown)`: This throws a specific exception.

- `thenAnswer(Answer answer)`: Unlike returning a specific value, some logic is executed and an action is taken from that logic; for example, some value is computed and returned. `Answer` is an interface.

- `thenCallRealMethod()`: This calls the real method on the object. The real method doesn't return any default value. It performs the actual logic, but if it needs to invoke any method that is stubbed, then the stubbed value is passed to the real method; for example, the `foo()` method calls `bar()`, but `bar()` is stubbed to return a value 10, so `foo()` will get 10.

The following test code stubs the `portfolio` and `marketWatcher` methods:

```
import com.packt.trading.dto.Stock;
import static org.junit.Assert.assertNotNull;
import static org.mockito.Matchers.anyString;
import static org.mockito.Matchers.isA;
import static org.mockito.Mockito.verify;
import static org.mockito.Mockito.when;

@RunWith(MockitoJUnitRunner.class)
public class StockBrokerTest {
   @Mock    MarketWatcher marketWatcher;
  @Mock    Portfolio portfolio;
   StockBroker broker;

   @Before public void setUp() {
    broker = new StockBroker(marketWatcher);
   }

   @Test
   public void when_ten_percent_gain_then_the_stock_is_sold() {
     //Portfolio's getAvgPrice is stubbed to return $10.00
    when(portfolio.getAvgPrice(isA(Stock.class))).
                  thenReturn(new BigDecimal("10.00"));
     //A stock object is created with current price $11.20
     Stock aCorp = new Stock("A", "A Corp", new
         BigDecimal("11.20"));
     //getQuote method is stubbed to return the stock
     when(marketWatcher.getQuote(anyString())).thenReturn(
         aCorp);
```

```
    //perform method is called, as the stock price increases
    // by 12% the broker should sell the stocks
    broker.perform(portfolio, aCorp);

    //verifying that the broker sold the stocks
    verify(portfolio).sell(aCorp,10);
}
```

The stubbed `getAvgPrice()` method returns `$10.00`, and the stubbed `getQuote` method returns a stock of `A Corp`. The stock is configured to return the current stock price as `$11.20`. As the current stock price (`$11.20`) is 12 percent more than the average stock price (`$10`), `broker` will sell 10 `A Corp` stocks to book profit.

We already know that the if we don't stub a method on a mock object, then that method returns a default value, but for the void methods, there is nothing to be returned, so no action is taken. In our case, the broker logic invokes the `sell` method on the portfolio object, but the `sell` method is a void method, so the `sell` method is auto-stubbed and it doesn't connect to the database to update the portfolio status. It simply dumps the call.

The `perform` method is a void method, so it doesn't return any response saying whether it sold some units or not. So how would we check the logic that 10 stocks were sold? We use `Mockito.verify`.

The `verify()` method is a static method. It is used to verify the method invocation. If we verify a method call on a mock object but the method is not invoked by the code logic, then the `verify()` method raises an exception to indicate that there is something wrong in the code logic. In the preceding example we verified that 10 stocks were sold, but if the code logic doesn't call the `sell` method due to some bug in logic and our test verifies the call in test, it signifies that the code is buggy.

Verifying in depth

An overloaded version of `verify()` takes `org.mockito.internal.verification.Times` as an argument. `Times` takes the `wantedNumberOfInvocations` integer argument.

When we pass 0 to `Times`, it means that the stubbed method has not been invoked in the testing path, but if the method is invoked once, then the `verify` method raises an exception. If we pass a negative number to the `Times` constructor, then it throws `MockitoException` - `org.mockito.exceptions.base.MockitoException`, and shows the **Negative value is not allowed here** error message.

The following methods can be used in combination with `verify`:

- `times(int wantedNumberOfInvocations)`: This signifies that the stubbed method was invoked exactly `wantedNumberOfInvocations` times. If the method invocation count doesn't match, then the test fails.

- `never()`: This is equivalent to `times(0)`. It signifies that the method wasn't invoked at all.

- `atLeastOnce()`: This signifies that the stubbed method was invoked at least once. It doesn't throw an error if the method is invoked multiple times, but fails if the method is not invoked.

- `atLeast(int minNumberOfInvocations)`: This signifies that the stubbed method was invoked `minNumberOfInvocations` or more times. It doesn't throw an error if the stubbed method is invoked more than `minNumberOfInvocations` times but fails if the stubbed method is invoked less than `minNumberOfInvocations` times.

- `atMost(int maxNumberOfInvocations)`: This signifies that the stubbed method was invoked `maxNumberOfInvocations` times. It raises an exception if the method is called more than `minNumberOfInvocations` times and works fine if the method is never invoked or invoked less than the maximum count.

- `only()`: This is the only method called on a mock. It fails if any other method is called on the mock object. In our example, if we use `verify(portfolio, only()).sell(aCorp, 10);`, the test will fail with following output:

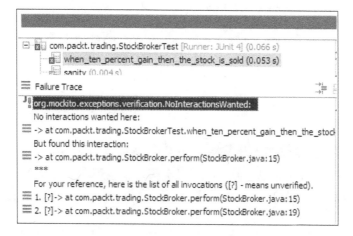

The test fails when, `portfolio.getAvgPrice(stock)` is called (in line number 15).

- `timeout(int millis)`: This interacts in a specified time range.

Verifying zero and no more interactions

The verifyZeroInteractions(object... mocks) method takes an array of mock objects and verifies that no methods were called on the mocks. This is important to check the logic branching. Suppose we have two sets of classes, one to send e-mails, and one to generate the mail printout to be sent over the general mail. During code execution, it should either send an e-mail or print a mail. For the e-mail path, we can verify that no methods were called on the mail printout classes.

The following test demonstrates the verifyZeroInteractions method and directly passes the two mock objects to it. Since no methods are invoked on the mock objects, the test passes:

```
@Test
public void verify_zero_interaction() {
    verifyZeroInteractions(marketWatcher,portfolio);
}
```

The verifyNoMoreInteractions(Object... mocks) method checks whether any of the given mocks has any unverified interaction. We can use this method after verifying a mock method to ensure that nothing else was invoked in the mock.

The following test code demonstrates the verifyNoMoreInteractions method:

```
@Test  public void verify_no_more_interaction() {
  Stock noStock = null;
   portfolio.getAvgPrice(noStock);
   portfolio.sell(null, 0);
   verify(portfolio).getAvgPrice(eq(noStock));
   //this will fail as the sell method was invoked
   verifyNoMoreInteractions(portfolio);
}
```

Here is a screenshot showing the JUnit output of the preceding code:

Throwing exceptions

When a piece of code throws a business exception due to violations of some core business logic, then the program should handle the exception instead of halting (for the errors such as Out Of Memory or disk failure, it should definitely halt). In our unit tests, we should consider exceptional conditions such as the code requesting to sell 10 stocks and the portfolio containing only five stocks. Mockito provides methods to throw exceptions during testing.

Mockito defines an action method called thenThrow(Throwable). This method throws a specific exception when a trigger occurs or a stubbed method is called.

The getAvgPrice method scans the database to fetch the average stock price. Suppose the database is unavailable for upgrade or some other reason, and you invoked the method. Then the getAvgPrice will throw an exception, but it is we who should handle the exception and show a proper meaningful error message to the user. We'll use Mockito's API to throw an exception from the getAvgPrice method:

```
@Test(expected = IllegalStateException.class)
public void throwsException() throws Exception {
  when(portfolio.getAvgPrice(isA(Stock.class))).thenThrow(
      new IllegalStateException("Database down"));

  portfolio.getAvgPrice(new Stock(null, null, null));
}
```

We stubbed the getAvgPrice method of portfolio to throw an exception.

The following is the syntax to throw an exception from a void method:

```
doThrow(exception).when(mock).voidmethod(arguments);
```

The buy method portfolio is a void method, so we'll stub it to throw an exception:

```
@Test(expected = IllegalStateException.class)
public void throwsException_void_methods() throws Exception {
  doThrow(new IllegalStateException()).
          when(portfolio).buy(isA(Stock.class));
  portfolio.buy(new Stock(null, null, null));
}
```

To learn advanced Mockito topics such as `Answers`, `ArgumentCaptor`, matchers, and so on, read the following books:

- *Mastering Unit Testing Using Mockito and JUnit, Sujoy Acharya* (`https://www.packtpub.com/application-development/mastering-unit-testing-using-mockito-and-junit`)
- *Mockito Essentials, Sujoy Acharya* (`https://www.packtpub.com/application-development/mockito-essentials`)

Summary

This JUnit refresher chapter covered both basic and advanced applications of JUnit. We also covered annotation-based JUnit testing, assertion, the `@RunWith` annotation, exception handling, setting up Eclipse for running JUnit tests, matchers, `assertThat`, and the custom `lessThanOrEqual()` matcher.

Then the Mockito framework was described in depth, and technical examples were provided to demonstrate the capability of Mockito.

The next chapter focuses on getting the reader quickly started with Spring Framework unit testing. It provides an overview of Spring integration testing and explores the test APIs.

3
Working with Spring Tests

This chapter covers the test module of Spring and the APIs used for unit and integration testing Spring applications. The following topics are covered here:

- Spring's `TestContext` framework and `SpringJUnit4ClassRunner`
- Spring profiles
- Mocking environments with `MockEnvironment` and `MockPropertySource`
- Mocking a JNDI lookup with `SimpleNamingContextBuilder` and `ExpectedLookupTemplate`
- Testing with `ReflectionTestUtils`
- Exploring Spring annotations for unit testing; the annotations covered are `@ContextConfiguration`, `ApplicationContextInitializer`, `@WebAppConfiguration`, `@ContextHierarchy`, `@ActiveProfiles`, `@ProfileValueSourceConfiguration`, `@TestPropertySource`, `@DirtiesContext`, `@TestExecutionListeners`, `@IfProfileValue`, `@Timed`, and `@Repeat`
- Unit testing Spring MVC with `MockHttpServletRequest`, `MockHttpSession`, and `ModelAndViewAssert`, as well as Spring beans with request scope and Spring beans with session scope
- Mocking a servlet container with `MockMvc`
- Transaction management with `@Transactional`, `@TransactionConfiguration`, `@Rollback`, `@BeforeTransaction`, and `@AfterTransaction`

Exploring the TestContext framework

Spring's TestContext framework is a generic, annotation-driven framework for unit and integration testing. The framework's resources are located in the org.springframework.test.context package. This framework believes in the design paradigm "convention over configuration," which means that the framework provides reasonable defaults for every configuration; the user can still override the unconventional aspects through annotation-based configuration. The TestContext framework provides support for JUnit and TestNG, such as a custom JUnit runner that allows non-invasive POJO test classes.

The framework consists of two classes and three interfaces. The following are the classes:

- TestContext: This class provides the context in which a test is executed. It also makes the context management and caching supports available for the test instance. To load the application context, the ContextLoader interface (or SmartContextLoader) is used.

- TestContextManager: This class is the main entry point to the TestContext framework; it manages a single TestContext class and publishes events to all registered TestExecutionListener implementations at test execution points. These are the test execution points:
  - In static before class methods
  - In before test execution methods
  - During test instance preparation
  - In after test execution methods
  - In static after class methods

The following are the interfaces:

- TestExecutionListener: The TestContextManager class publishes events to all the registered listeners. This interface defines the listener API to react to the published events.

- ContextLoader: This interface loads ApplicationContext for the Spring integration tests.

- SmartContextLoader: This interface is the extension of the ContextLoader interface and has been introduced in Spring 3.1. A SmartContextLoader interface processes resource locations, annotated classes, or context initializers. Also, it can set active bean profiles (@ActiveProfiles) and property sources in the context that it loads.

For each test, a `TestContextManager` class is being created. The `TestContextManager` class handles a `TestContext` class for the current test and updates the state of the `TestContext` class as the test progresses. For dependency injection, dirty checks, transactional support, and so on, the `TestContextManager` class delegates control to the `TestExecutionListener` implementations, which in turn implements the actual test execution by providing dependency injection, managing transactions, and so on.

The default `TestExecutionListener` implementations are registered in the following order:

- `ServletTestExecutionListener`: This listener provides the Servlet API mocks for `WebApplicationContext`
- `DependencyInjectionTestExecutionListener`: As the name suggests, this listener provides dependency injections for the test
- `DirtiesContextTestExecutionListener`: This listener checks the context—whether any bean is dirtied or not during a test execution; it also handles the `@DirtiesContext` annotation
- `TransactionalTestExecutionListener`: This provides transactional support
- `SqlScriptsTestExecutionListener`: This executes SQL scripts configured via the `@Sql` annotation

The `TestExecutionListener` implementations externalize the reusable code to instrument tests. When we execute a `TestExecutionListener` implementation, we can reuse it across test class hierarchies and projects. Custom `TestExecutionListener` implementations can be registered for a test class and its subclasses via the `@TestExecutionListeners` annotation. If a custom `TestExecutionListener` implementation is registered via `@TestExecutionListeners`, the default listeners will not be registered. As a result, the developer has to manually declare all the default listeners in addition to any custom listeners. The following example demonstrates this style of configuration. Usually, we don't need a custom `TestExecutionListener` implementation unless we want to perform some custom logic before, during, or after the test method or test class execution. In the following section, we'll create a custom listener to print the test class and method names just before and after test execution.

Writing a custom TestExecutionListener interface

The following are the steps to create a custom `TestExecutionListener` implementation:

1. Create a Java project, `SpringTests`.

2. Create a `SysOutTestExecutionListener` Java class in the `com.packt.listener` package and implement the `TestExecutionListener` interface. All implemented methods print information about the test class or the test method. The `TestExecutionListener` listener can be reused with any Spring test class. The following is the implementation:

```
public class SysOutTestExecutionListener implements
        TestExecutionListener {
@Override public void afterTestClass(TestContext
        testContext) throws Exception {
  ApplicationContext ctx =
        testContext.getApplicationContext();
  System.out.println("In afterTestClass for class =
        "+testContext.getTestClass());
}
```

Note that you can get the application context, `ctx`, from the `TestContext` class to work with the Spring beans. Although I'm not doing any alterations to any bean configuration, you can do so from all the methods in a `TestExecutionListner` class, as shown here:

```
@Override public void afterTestMethod(TestContext testContext)
        throws Exception {
  System.out.println("In afterTestMethod for =
        "+testContext.getTestMethod().getName());
}
@Override public void beforeTestClass(TestContext
        testContext) throws Exception {
  System.out.println("In beforeTestClass for class =
        "+testContext.getTestClass());
}
@Override public void beforeTestMethod(TestContext
        testContext) throws Exception {
  System.out.println("In beforeTestMethod for =
        "+testContext.getTestMethod().getName());
}
```

```
@Override
public void prepareTestInstance(TestContext testContext)
      throws Exception {
   System.out.println("In prepareTestInstance for=
      "+testContext.getTestInstance());
}
}
```

The `SysOutTestExecutionListener` class implements five methods, namely, `afterTestClass`, `beforeTestClass`, `afterTestMethod`, `beforeTestMethod`, and `prepareTestInstance`. Each method accepts a `TestContext` object. A `TextContext` object can provide the test method, test class, test instance, application context, and the beans configured in the application context, and so on. We'll check the method execution sequence later.

3. Create an empty `applicationContext.xml` file directly under the `com.packt.listener` package. You don't need to define any bean here. The following is the XML file:

    ```
    <?xml version="1.0" encoding="UTF-8"?>
    <beans
        xmlns="http://www.springframework.org/schema/beans"
      xmlns:xsi="http://www.w3.org/2001/XMLSchema-instance"
      xsi:schemaLocation=
      "http://www.springframework.org/schema/beans
      http://www.springframework.org/schema/beans/spring-
            beans.xsd">
    </beans>
    ```

4. Create a test class to examine `SysOutTestExecutionListener`. The class details are as follows:

    ```
    package com.packt.listener;

    import org.junit.Test;
    import org.junit.runner.RunWith;
    import org.springframework.test.context.ContextConfiguration;
    import org.springframework.test.context.TestExecutionListeners;
    import org.springframework.test.context.junit4.
    SpringJUnit4ClassRunner;

    @RunWith(SpringJUnit4ClassRunner.class)
    @ContextConfiguration(locations="classpath:com/packt/listener/
    applicationContext.xml")
    @TestExecutionListeners({
        SysOutTestExecutionListener.class
    ```

```
})
public class TestExecutionListenerTest {

  @Test
  public void someTest() throws Exception {
    System.out.println("executing someTest");
  }

  @Test
  public void someOtherTest() throws Exception {
    System.out.println("executing someOtherTest");
  }
}
```

The class is annotated with `@RunWith`, `@ContextConfiguration`, and `@ TestExecutionListeners`. By annotating test classes with `@RunWith(SpringJUnit4ClassRunner.class)`, we enable the class to get the benefits of Spring unit and integration tests, such as `TestContext`, the `applicationContext` loading, DI, transaction support, and so on.

The `@ContextConfiguration` annotation loads the application context resource from the specified `locations` or the `@Configuration` annotated classes. In `locations`, we pass the XML configuration or the `applicationContext` XML location that can be loaded from the classpath.

The `@TestExecutionListeners` annotation defines class-level metadata to configure which `TestExecutionListener` implementations should be registered with `TestContextManager`.

5. The `TestExecutionListenerTest` class has two tests. When we execute the test class, the following output is displayed:

In **beforeTestClass** for class = class com.packt.listener.
TestExecutionListenerTest

In **prepareTestInstance** for= com.packt.listener.TestExecutionListen
erTest@548c491e

In **beforeTestMethod** for = someOtherTest

executing someOtherTest

In **afterTestMethod** for = someOtherTest

In **prepareTestInstance** for= com.packt.listener.TestExecutionListen
erTest@5cd99967

In **beforeTestMethod** for = someTest

executing someTest

In **afterTestMethod** for = someTest

In **afterTestClass** for class = class com.packt.listener.
TestExecutionListenerTest

The `beforeTestClass` method is invoked first, and it is invoked only once for the test class; we can access the application context and beans using this method. The `prepareTestMethod` is invoked before any test method execution. We can get the test instance and prepare beans or initialize test-specific data from this method. The `beforeTestMethod` is executed after `prepareTestMethod` but before any test method execution, and then a test is executed. The `afterTestMethod` is executed after any test method execution. The `afterTestClass` method acts like the destructors in C++, and is invoked only once per class at the end of the last test method's `afterTestMethod` call.

You might wonder what the difference is between JUnit 4's `@before` and `@after` and the `TestExecutionListener` methods. The answer is you can access `TestContext` in the `TestExecutionListener` methods but not in JUnit annotated methods, and `TestExecutionListener` logic can be shared with many tests but JUnit annotations are test class specific. For example, our `SysOutTestExecutionListener` logic can be shared with any test class; but if we annotate a test method with a JUnit 4 annotation, then that method cannot be shared with all the test classes unless they extend the class.

6. If a custom `TestExecutionListener` class is registered via `@TestExecutionListeners`, the default listeners will not be registered. This forces the developer to manually declare all default listeners in addition to any custom listeners. The following listing demonstrates this style of configuration:

```
@ContextConfiguration
@TestExecutionListeners({
    SysOutTestExecutionListener.class,
    ServletTestExecutionListener.class,

    DependencyInjectionTestExecutionListener.class,

    DirtiesContextTestExecutionListener.class,

    TransactionalTestExecutionListener.class,

    SqlScriptsTestExecutionListener.class
})
public class TestExecutionListenerTest {

}
```

7. To avoid the redeclaration of all default listeners, the `mergeMode` attribute of `@TestExecutionListeners` can be set to `MergeMode.MERGE_WITH_DEFAULTS`. The `MERGE_WITH_DEFAULTS` part indicates that locally declared listeners should be merged with the default listeners, as shown in the following listing:

```
@ContextConfiguration
@TestExecutionListeners(
    listeners = SysOutTestExecutionListener.class,
    mergeMode = MERGE_WITH_DEFAULTS

)
public class TestExecutionListenerTest {

}
```

The `TextContext` framework does not force you to extend any particular class or to implement a specific interface in order to configure the application context. Instead, configuration is achieved simply by declaring the `@ContextConfiguration` annotation at the class level.

Configuring Spring profiles

Spring 3.1 introduced a feature called profiles. Profiles allow you to build one package that can be deployed in all environments, such as dev, test, prod, perf, and so on.

If we define a system property, `spring.profiles.active`, or annotate a test class with `@ActiveProfiles` and set the active profile names, Spring loads the beans from the context where the profile name matches or no profile name is defined. We can create different beans depending on the profile name using an XML configuration or the `@Profile` annotation.

Suppose you have a dev environment and a prod environment; you use a JNDI lookup for `DataSource` in prod, but in dev, you build `DataSource`, as in the following snippet:

```
<jee:jndi-lookup id="common-Datasource" jndi-name="java:comp/env/
Datasource"
    resource-ref="true" cache="true" lookup-on-startup="false"
    proxy-interface="javax.sql.DataSource" />
```

In dev, we redefine it as follows:

```xml
<bean id="common-Datasource"
   class="org.springframework.jdbc.datasource
           .DriverManagerDataSource"
     autowire-candidate="false"
     >

     <property name="driverClassName"
         value="${jdbc.driverClassName}" />
     <property name="url" value="${jdbc.url}"/>
     <property name="username" value="${jdbc.username}"/>
     <property name="password" value="${jdbc.password}"/>
</bean>
```

We need to load the DataSource bean depending on the environment. In a dev environment, the second bean should be loaded, and in prod, the first `<jee>` definition should be loaded.

The following are the steps to examine the profile feature:

1. Create a `com.packt.profile` package and an `applicationContext.xml` file and define three beans. The following is the body of the XML file:

    ```xml
    <beans >
        <bean name="noProfileBean" id="noProfileBean"
            class="java.lang.String">
            <constructor-arg value="I'm a free bean" />
        </bean>

        <beans profile="dev">
            <bean name="message" id="message" class="java.lang.String">
            <constructor-arg value="I'm a dev bean" />
        </bean>
        </beans>

        <beans profile="prod">
            <bean name="message" id="message" class="java.lang.String">
            <constructor-arg value="I'm a prod bean" />
        </bean>
        </beans>
    </beans>
    ```

We defined two profiles, `prod` and `dev`, and in each profile we defined a String bean message, but the content of the message is different in the two profiles. We also defined a `noProfileBean` String bean directly under the default beans with no profile name.

2. Create a test class to load the `dev` profile context and assert the message bean value to check that the `dev` profile value is loaded. The following is the test:

```
package com.packt.profile;
import org.springframework.test.context.ActiveProfiles;
@RunWith(SpringJUnit4ClassRunner.class)
@ContextConfiguration(locations="classpath:com/packt/profile/
applicationContext.xml")
@ActiveProfiles(profiles={"dev"})
public class ProfileTest {
  @Autowired
      ApplicationContext context;
  @Test
  public void profile() throws Exception {
    assertEquals("I'm a dev bean",
        context.getBean("message"));
    assertEquals("I'm a free bean",
        context.getBean("noProfileBean"));
  }
}
```

The `@ActiveProfiles` annotation takes an array of active profile names. We passed the value `dev` to load the `dev` profile beans. We asserted the message bean value with `I'm a dev bean`. Note that the `noProfileBean` is also loaded with the value `I'm a free bean` although we asked to load the `dev` profile. When we define a bean in the absence of a profile name (or just under the default profile) and try to load a specific profile, the bean defined under no profile is also loaded along with the beans with matching profile names.

If we change the `@ActiveProfiles` annotation to load both the profiles, such as `@ActiveProfiles(profiles={"dev", "prod"})`, the Spring context loads the last defined bean in the application context, as the `prod` profile is defined after the `dev` profile (in `applictionContext.xml`). So, here it will load the `prod` profile bean and the test will fail, as the test asserts the `dev` value with a `prod` value.

The following is the failure stack:

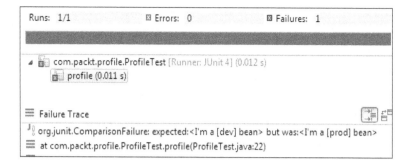

In the test, if you change the sequence as `@ActiveProfiles(profiles={"pr od", "dev"})`, the test will also fail as the order is defined in the XML file.

3. Now, remove the `@ActiveProfiles` annotation, open the Eclipse JUnit run configuration, go to the **Environment** tab, and define a `spring.profiles.active = dev` variable. Rerun the test, and it will pass:

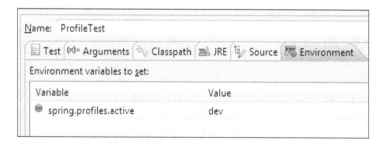

The `@ActiveProfiles` annotation is used in tests to load a specific profile(s); in web/standalone applications, the following environment variable approach is used:

```
-Dspring.profiles.active= profile1, profile2 ...
```

Mocking an environment

The `Environment` interface and the `PropertySource` class were added to Spring 3.1 in order to simplify working with properties. In Spring 3.2, `MockEnvironment` and `MockPropertySource` were added to the mock properties in tests. We'll create a program to configure a bean from a properties file value and then mock out the properties file value with `MockEnvironment` and `MockPropertySource`.

The following are the steps:

1. Create a `myProp.properties` properties file under the `test` source folder and add the following property:

   ```
   message = I'm the king
   ```

2. You can define a Spring configuration context by annotating a class with the `@Configuration` annotation. The `@PropertySource` annotation takes the properties' filenames and sets the properties to the `Environment` resource. Create a `MyConfig` configuration class under the `com.packt.environment` package. The following is the configuration class:

   ```
   @Configuration
   @PropertySource({"classpath:myProp.properties"})
   public class MyConfig {

     @Resource
     private Environment environment;

     @Bean(name="message")
       public String getMessage() {
       return new environment.getProperty("message");
       }
   }
   ```

   A `message` String bean is defined with the `@Bean` annotation, and the String bean is initialized from the `message` property value defined in the `myProp.properties` file.

3. Create a test class to load the message bean from the application context and assert the bean value with `I'm the king`:

   ```
   @RunWith(SpringJUnit4ClassRunner.class)
   @ContextConfiguration(classes=MyConfig.class)
   public class EnvironmentTest {

     @Autowired
     ApplicationContext context;
     @Test
     public void environment() throws Exception {
       assertEquals("I'm the king", context.getBean("message"));
     }
   }
   ```

   The `@ContextConfiguration` annotation takes the `@Configuration` class name to load the context. The test passes as the configuration class initializes the bean with the property value.

4. Suppose we want to mock the properties file reading with a mock value. To mock the `Environment` value, we need to change the application context's `Environment` value at the time of context initialization. The `@ContextConfiguration` annotation takes a `ApplicationContextInitializer` instance for explicit initialization; we can create a `ApplicationContextInitializer` instance and change the `Environment` value of `ApplicationContext` with a `MockEnvironment` object. The following is the modified test:

```
@RunWith(SpringJUnit4ClassRunner.class)
@ContextConfiguration(classes=MyConfig.class, initializers
        = EnvironmentTest.MockPropertyInitializer.class)
public class EnvironmentTest {

  @Autowired
  ApplicationContext context;
  @Test
  public void environment() throws Exception {
    assertEquals("I'm the king",
          context.getBean("message"));
  }

  public static class MockPropertyInitializer implements
        ApplicationContextInitializer
          <ConfigurableApplicationContext> {

    @Override
    public void initialize(ConfigurableApplicationContext
        applicationContext) {
      MockEnvironment mock = new MockEnvironment();
      mock.setProperty("message", "I'm a mockstar");
      applicationContext.setEnvironment(mock);
    }
  }
}
```

Here, `MockPropertyInitializer` implements the
`ApplicationContextInitializer` instance and replaces `Environment` of
`applicationContext` with `MockEnvironment`. The `@ContextConfigura`
`tion(classes=MyConfig.class, initializers = EnvironmentTest.`
`MockPropertyInitializer.class)` annotation invokes the
`MockPropertyInitializer` instance at the time of initialization and
sets the `message` property with the value `I'm a mockstar`. When we
run the test, the assertion fails with the expectation `I'm a mockstar`:

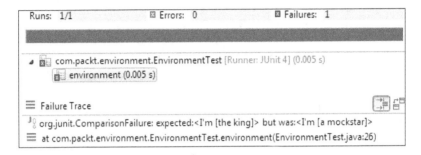

5. Similarly, we can use `MockPropertySource` with a mock value to
   mock out the properties file values. The following is the modified
   `MockPropertyInitializer`:

```
public static class MockPropertyInitializer implements
        ApplicationContextInitializer
            <ConfigurableApplicationContext> {

    @Override
    public void initialize(ConfigurableApplicationContext
            applicationContext) {
      MutablePropertySources propertySources =
          applicationContext.getEnvironment()
            .getPropertySources();
      MockPropertySource mockEnvVars = new MockPropertySource()
          .withProperty("message", "I'm a mock");
      propertySources.replace(StandardEnvironment.
          SYSTEM_ENVIRONMENT_PROPERTY_SOURCE_NAME,
            mockEnvVars);
        }
}
```

Here, we get a `MutablePropertySources` class from the `Environment` value of
`applicationContext` and then replace the `SYSTEM_ENVIRONMENT_PROPERTY_`
`SOURCE_NAME` of `MutablePropertySources` with `MockPropertySource`.

Mocking the JNDI lookup

Sometimes, we need to mock the `<jee:jndi-lookup>`/JNDI lookup with a mock value in the out-of-container tests. The `org.springframework.mock.jndi` package contains an implementation of the JNDI SPI, which you can use to set up a simple JNDI environment for test suites or standalone applications. In the following example, we'll define `<jee:jndi-lookup>` for the `DataSource` resource in `applicationContext` and mock out the lookup from the test. The following are the steps to mock up a JNDI call:

1. Create an `applicationContext.xml` file in the `com.packt.jndi` package, with the following details:

```
<?xml version="1.0" encoding="UTF-8"?>
<beans xmlns="http://www.springframework.org/schema/beans"
    xmlns:jee="http://www.springframework.org/schema/jee"
    xmlns:xsi="http://www.w3.org/2001/XMLSchema-instance"
   xsi:schemaLocation="
http://www.springframework.org/schema/beans http://www.
springframework.org/schema/beans/spring-beans.xsd
http://www.springframework.org/schema/jee
http://www.springframework.org/schema/jee/spring-jee-4.1.xsd
">


<jee:jndi-lookup id="common-Datasource"
            jndi-name="java:comp/env/Datasource"
    resource-ref="true" cache="true"
            lookup-on-startup="false"
    proxy-interface="javax.sql.DataSource" />


</beans>
```

2. When we run a JUnit test, the container is not accessible; hence, we need to mock out the `<jee:jndi-lookup>` from our JUnit test. We'll create an `ApplicationContextInitializer` instance to initialize the application context and bind a mock `DataSource` object with the original `DataSource` name. The following is the test code:

```
@RunWith(SpringJUnit4ClassRunner.class)
@ContextConfiguration(locations = "classpath:com/packt/jndi/
applicationContext.xml",
    initializers =
```

```
        DataSourceTest.MockJeeLookUpInitializer.class)
public class DataSourceTest {

  @Autowired
  ApplicationContext context;

  @Test
  public void jndiResource() throws Exception {
    assertNotNull(context.getBean("common-Datasource"));
  }

  public static class MockJeeLookUpInitializer implements
      ApplicationContextInitializer
        <ConfigurableApplicationContext> {

  @Override
  public void initialize(
    ConfigurableApplicationContext applicationContext) {
      DataSource mockDataSource = (javax.sql.DataSource)
          Mockito.mock(javax.sql.DataSource.class);
      SimpleNamingContextBuilder builder = new
          SimpleNamingContextBuilder();
      builder.bind("java:comp/env/Datasource",
          mockDataSource);
       try {
        builder.activate();
      } catch (IllegalStateException |
           NamingException e) {
        e.printStackTrace();
      }
    }
   }
  }
}
```

A `SimpleNamingContextBuilder` object is created and then a mock `DataSource` object is bound to the name java:comp/env/Datasource; finally, the builder is activated in the `ApplicationContextInitializer` interface.

Using ReflectionTestUtils

The `org.springframework.test.util` package contains `ReflectionTestUtils`, which is a collection of reflection-based utility methods to set a non-public field or invoke a private/protected setter method when testing the application code, as follows:

- ORM frameworks, such as JPA and Hibernate, condone private or protected field access as opposed to public setter methods for properties in a domain entity

- Spring's support for annotations such as `@Autowired`, `@Inject`, and `@Resource`, which provide dependency injections for private or protected fields, setter methods, and configuration methods

The following example demonstrates the capabilities of `ReflectionUtils`:

1. Create a `Secret` class in the `com.packt.testutils` package with a private String field, `secret`, and a public method, `initiate`, to encrypt a String and set it to `secret`. The following is the class:

```
package com.packt.testutils;

public class Secret {
  private String secret;

  public void initiate(String key) {
    this.secret = key.replaceAll("a", "z")
        .replaceAll("i", "k");
  }
}
```

The `initiate` method replaces all the instances of a with z and all the instances of i with k. So, if you pass `aio` to the method, `zko` will be set to `secret`.

2. The following test class invokes the `getField` and `setField` methods of `ReflectionUtils` to access the private field of the `Secret` class:

```
package com.packt.testutils;

import static org.junit.Assert.*;

import java.lang.reflect.Field;

import org.junit.Test;
import org.springframework.util.ReflectionUtils;
```

```
public class ReflectionUtilsTest {

    @Test
    public void private_field_access() throws Exception {
        Secret myClass = new Secret();
        myClass.initiate("aio");
        Field secretField =
            ReflectionUtils.findField(Secret.class,
                "secret", String.class);
        assertNotNull(secretField);
        ReflectionUtils.makeAccessible(secretField);
        assertEquals("zko",
            ReflectionUtils.getField(secretField, myClass));

        ReflectionUtils.setField(secretField, myClass,
            "cool");
        assertEquals("cool",
            ReflectionUtils.getField(secretField, myClass));
    }
}
```

First, it finds the `secret` field and makes it accessible; then, it calls the `getField` method to access the `private` field value, and finally the `setField` method is called to set a new value to the `private` field.

Working with annotations

The Spring Framework provides a set of Spring-specific annotations for unit and integration tests in conjunction with the `TestContext` framework. The following are widely used annotations:

- `@ContextConfiguration`: We have already covered this annotation and loaded `applicationContext` for integration tests. This annotation is used to determine how to load and configure an `ApplicationContext` for integration tests. `@ContextConfiguration` declares the application context's resource locations or the annotated classes that will be used to load the context.

- `@WebAppConfiguration`: This class-level annotation is used to instruct the Spring context that the `ApplicationContext` loaded using the `@ContextConfiguration` annotation is a `WebApplicationContext`. We will use `WebApplicationContext` in the next section.

- @ContextHierarchy: This is a class-level annotation that loads the parent-child application context in hierarchical order. The following integration test declares a context hierarchy of two levels, one for the root WebApplicationContext (loaded using the TestConfig class) and one for the dispatcher servlet WebApplicationContext (loaded using the WebConfig class). The WebApplicationContext that is autowired into the test instance is the one used for the child context:

```
@RunWith(SpringJUnit4ClassRunner.class)
@WebAppConfiguration
@ContextHierarchy({
    @ContextConfiguration(classes = TestConfig.class),
    @ContextConfiguration(classes = WebConfig.class)
})
public class IntegrationTests {

    @Autowired
    private WebApplicationContext wac;

    // ...
}
```

- @ActiveProfiles: This class-level annotation is used to instruct the bean container about which bean definition profiles should be active during application context loading. The following example instructs the container to load the dev and test profiles:

```
@ContextConfiguration
@ActiveProfiles({"dev", "test"})
public class MyTest {

}
```

- @TestPropertySource: This class-level annotation is used to configure the locations of the properties files and the inline properties to be added to the set of PropertySources of Environment during ApplicationContext loading. The following example loads a property from the classpath:

```
@ContextConfiguration
@TestPropertySource("/test.properties")
public class MyTest {
    // class body...
}
```

- @DirtiesContext: This annotation specifies that the ApplicationContext has been dirtied during the execution of a test (such as, it changed the state of a singleton bean) and should be closed. When an application context is dirtied, it is removed from the testing framework's cache and closed. This annotation can be used as both a class- and method-level within the same test class.

- @TestExecutionListeners: We have already covered this class-level annotation before.

- @Timed: This method-level annotation indicates that the annotated test method must finish execution in a specified time period (in milliseconds). If the text execution time exceeds the specified time period, the test fails. The following is an example of @Timed:

```
@Timed(millis=2000)
public void testTwoSecondsTimeout() {
    // some logic that should not take longer than 2 seconds to
execute
}
```

- @Repeat: This method-level annotation indicates that the test method must be executed repeatedly. The number of times the test method is to be executed is specified in the annotation:

```
@Repeat(100)
@Test
public void testToBeRepeated() {
    // ...
}
```

Testing Spring MVC

This section will mock the request and session scope beans with MockHttpServletRequest and MockHttpSession:

1. Create a dynamic web project, SpringWebTest, add the Spring-mvc jars to the classpath, and modify the web.xml file (stored under <project>/WebContent/WEB-INF/) to enable Spring DispatcherServlet as follows:

```
<?xml version="1.0" encoding="UTF-8"?>
<web-app xmlns:xsi="http://www.w3.org/2001/XMLSchema-instance"
xmlns="http://java.sun.com/xml/ns/javaee" xmlns:web="http://java.
sun.com/xml/ns/javaee/web-app_2_5.xsd" xsi:schemaLocation="http://
java.sun.com/xml/ns/javaee http://java.sun.com/xml/ns/javaee/web-
app_3_0.xsd" id="WebApp_ID" version="3.0">
  <display-name>SpringWebTest</display-name>
```

```xml
  <servlet>
   <servlet-name>dispatcher</servlet-name>
   <servlet-class>
     org.springframework.web.servlet.DispatcherServlet
   </servlet-class>
   <load-on-startup>1</load-on-startup>
  </servlet>
  <servlet-mapping>
   <servlet-name>dispatcher</servlet-name>
   <url-pattern>/</url-pattern>
  </servlet-mapping>
  <context-param>
   <param-name>contextConfigLocation</param-name>
   <param-value>
     /WEB-INF/dispatcher-servlet.xml
   </param-value>
  </context-param>
</web-app>
```

2. Create a `LoginService` Java class in the `com.packt.controller` package to set the user ID and password and then validate them. The following is the class:

```java
public class LoginService {
  private String userId;
  private String password;
  //ignoring getters and setters for brevity
  public boolean isValid(){
    return getPassword().equals(getUserId());
  }
}
```

The `isValid()` method returns `true` when the username and password match.

3. Create a `LoginDetails` class in the `com.packt.controller` package to store the user ID and the first login time. The following is the class:

```java
public class LoginDetails {

private String user;
private Date loginTime;

public LoginDetails(String user, Date loginTime) {
  this.user = user;
  this.loginTime = loginTime;
```

```
    }

    public String getUser() {
      return user;
    }

    public Date getLoginTime() {
      return loginTime;
    }
}
```

4. Create a `Controller` class to handle requests. We'll have three requests: the initial request `"/"` will load the login page, the login page submit will invoke the `"/onLogin"` request, and validate the user ID and password. If the login is invalid, route the user to the login page; otherwise, store the user ID and login time in the session and pass the request to the `greetings` page. On the `greetings` page, the user can click on the `Login details` hyperlink to view the login time and user ID, and this will generate a `"/onLoginDetail"` request and get the login details from the session. The controller will be dependent on `LoginService` to get the user ID and password from the request and validate them, and on `LoginDetails` to fetch the user ID and login time from the session. The following is the controller:

```
@Controller
@Scope("session")
public class LoginController implements Serializable {
    @Autowired
    private LoginService loginService;

    @Autowired
    private LoginDetails loginDetails;

    @RequestMapping({ "/", "/login" })
    public String onStartUp(ModelMap model) {
      return "login";
    }

    @RequestMapping({ "/onLogin" })
    public ModelAndView onLogin(ModelMap model, HttpSession
          session, HttpServletRequest request) {
      if (!loginService.isValid()) {
        model.addAttribute("error", "Invalid user
            name and password");
        return new ModelAndView("login", model);
      }
```

```
session.setAttribute("loggedInTime", new Date());
session.setAttribute("userId",
        request.getParameter("userId"));

model.addAttribute("name", "Welcome reader!");
return new ModelAndView("greetings", model);
}


@RequestMapping({ "/onLoginDetail" })
public String onLoginDetail(ModelMap model) {
    model.addAttribute("name",
        loginDetails.getUser());
    model.addAttribute("time",
        loginDetails.getLoginTime());
    return "greetings";
}


}
```

5. Add an application context, dispatcher-servlet.xml, to define the beans. The loginService bean is defined in the request scope, and its properties are set from the request parameters using the p namespace. The loginDetails bean is defined in the session scope, and its constructor arguments are set from the session attributes using the c namespace:

```
<bean id="loginService"
        class="com.packt.controller.LoginService"
    scope="request"
        p:userId="#{request.getParameter('userId')}"
    p:password="#{request.getParameter('password')}">
    <aop:scoped-proxy />
</bean>
```

The <aop:scoped-proxy> is used to expand the scope of the beans:

```
<bean id="loginDetails"
        class="com.packt.controller.LoginDetails"
    c:user="#{session.getAttribute('userId')}"
      c:loginTime="#{session.getAttribute('loggedInTime')}"
    scope="session">
    <aop:scoped-proxy />
</bean>
```

```
<context:component-scan base-package="com.packt" />
<bean
class="org.springframework.web.servlet.view.
```

```
        InternalResourceViewResolver">
  <property name="prefix">
    <value>/WEB-INF/pages/</value>
  </property>
  <property name="suffix">
    <value>.jsp</value>
  </property>
</bean>
```

Also, the view resolver tells the Spring container to resolve the views from the /WEB-INF/pages folder with the .jsp suffix. This means that if the controller returns a view named greetings, then resolve the logical view to a physical greetings.jsp page under the /WEB-INF/pages folder.

6. How can we get the session and request scope beans in our JUnit test and set the request and session attributes? The following test class autowires the request-scoped LoginService and session-scoped LoginDetails; it also verifies the logic that isValid() checks the username and password, and the session attributes are properly passed to LoginDetails:

```
@RunWith(SpringJUnit4ClassRunner.class)
@ContextConfiguration(locations ="classpath:beans.xml")
@WebAppConfiguration
public class LoginControllerTest {
  @Autowired
  private LoginService loginService;
  @Autowired
  private LoginDetails loginDetails;
  @Autowired MockHttpServletRequest request;
  @Autowired MockHttpSession session;

  @Test
  public void requestScope() throws Exception {
    request.setParameter("userId", "rock");
      request.setParameter("password", "rock");

      assertTrue(loginService.isValid());
  }

  @Test
  public void sessionScope() throws Exception {
    Date now = new Date();
    session.setAttribute("userId", "john");
    session.setAttribute("loggedInTime", now);
```

```
    assertEquals("john",loginDetails.getUser());
    assertEquals(now,loginDetails.getLoginTime());
  }
}
```

The following things took place in the preceding test:

- We loaded a WebApplicationContext for our test by annotating the test class with @WebAppConfiguration

- We injected the mock request or session into our test instance and prepared test data as appropriate, such as setting the request parameters and session attributes

- We invoked the web component from the configured WebApplicationContext via dependency injections, and asserted the values against the mocks

Mocking the servlet container with MockMvc

The design behind the Spring MVC test is to test the controller by performing actual requests and generating responses, as they would be at runtime. MockMvc is used to mock the servlet container, and it can perform a request and verify the resulting response status and response elements. We'll build a Spring controller to generate a JSON response as in the case of a rest controller and then use MockMvc to unit test the request and the response:

1. Create a serializable Employee POJO class that holds employee information, such as ID, name, and salary.

2. Create a controller to return a specific employee and all employees with / employees/{id} and /employees/ urls. We'll create a HashMap and store dummy employees. The following is the class:

```
@Controller
public class HRController {
  private Map<Integer, Employee> database = new HashMap<Integer,
      Employee>();
  public HRController() {
    loadDummyData();
  }
  private void loadDummyData() {
    Employee john = new Employee();
    john.setId(1);
    john.setName("John Doe");
```

```
    john.setSalary(100.00);
    database.put(1, john);
    Employee karen = new Employee();
    karen.setId(2);
    karen.setName("Karen Cushing");
    karen.setSalary(500.00);
    database.put(2, karen);
}

@RequestMapping(value = "/employees/{id}", method =
        RequestMethod.GET)
public @ResponseBody
Employee retrieve(@PathVariable int id) {
  return database.get(id);
}

@RequestMapping(value = "/employees", method =
        RequestMethod.GET)
public @ResponseBody
List<Employee> retrieveAll() {
  return new ArrayList<Employee>(database.values());
}

}
```

Note that the `retrieve` and `retrieveAll` methods are annotated
with `@RequestMapping(value = "/employees/{id}", method =
RequestMethod.GET)` and `@RequestMapping(value = "/employees",
method = RequestMethod.GET)`, respectively to map the URLs. Also, both
the methods are annotated with an `@ResponseBody` annotation to return
response as JSON object.

3. When we run the web application and open the explorer to load the
`http://localhost:8080/SpringWebTest/employees/` URL, the
following JSON output is displayed:

```
[{"name":"John Doe","id":1,"salary":100.0},
{"name":"Karen Cushing","id":2,"salary":500.0}]
```

4. When we type `http://localhost:8080/SpringWebTest/employees/1`, this is how the output looks:

```
← → C    localhost:8080/SpringWebTest/employees/1

{"name":"John Doe","id":1,"salary":100.0}
```

5. We can examine the integration of the web tier with other tiers in isolation from a web container using the `org.springframework.test.web.servlet.MockMvc`, `org.springframework.test.web.servlet.request.MockMvcRequestBuilders`, and `org.springframework.test.web.servlet.result.MockMvcResultMatchers` classes. The following JUnit test demonstrates the usages of `MockMvc`:

```java
@RunWith(SpringJUnit4ClassRunner.class)
@ContextConfiguration(locations ="classpath:beans.xml")
@WebAppConfiguration
public class HRControllerTest {
  @Autowired
    private WebApplicationContext wac;
    private MockMvc mockMvc;

    @Before  public void setup() {
        this.mockMvc =
        MockMvcBuilders.webAppContextSetup
            (this.wac).build();
    }

    @Test public void getEmployee() throws Exception {
    this.mockMvc.perform(get("/employees/1").
    accept(MediaType.parseMediaType(
        "application/json;charset=UTF-8")))
            .andExpect(status().isOk())
            .andExpect(content().contentType(
                "application/json;charset=UTF-8"))
            .andExpect(jsonPath("$.name").value("John
                Doe"))
            .andExpect(jsonPath("$.salary").value(100.00))
            .andExpect(jsonPath("$.id").value(1));
    }
}
```

The `MockMvcBuilders` class needs a `WebApplicationContext` to build a `MockMvc` object; the `WebApplicationContext` is autowired using the `@WebAppConfiguration` annotation. The `MockMvc` object is used to perform a `GET` request to `/employees/1` and then it verifies that the response status is 200 (`isOk()`) as well as the JSON response. The `jsonPath("$.name").value("John Doe")` statement checks whether the output JSON contains a name field and its value is `John Doe`. So, we just bypassed the servlet container to test the real request/response handling.

Handling transactions in Spring tests

Spring provides a module/utility library for integration tests. The following are the steps to write JUnit tests using the Spring transaction management API and `SpringJUnit4ClassRunner`.

We'll reuse the `DataAccess` project used in *Chapter 1, Getting Familiar with the Spring Framework*.

1. Create a source folder, `integration`, directly under the `DataAccess` project. Spring supports XML-based configuration and wiring beans. Create an XML file, `integration.xml`, in the `integration` source package. Modify the XML and define the `dataSourceBean`, `transactionManagerBean`, and `JdbcTemplateBean` Spring beans. The following is the XML body:

```
<beans xmlns="http://www.springframework.org/schema/beans"
  xmlns:xsi="http://www.w3.org/2001/XMLSchema-instance"
  xsi:schemaLocation="
http://www.springframework.org/schema/beans
http://www.springframework.org/schema/beans/spring-beans-4.1.xsd">

  <bean id="dataSourceBean"
    class="org.springframework.jdbc.datasource.
      DriverManagerDataSource">
      <property name="driverClassName"
      value="org.apache.derby.jdbc.EmbeddedDriver"/>
      <property name="url"
      value="jdbc:derby:derbyDB;create=true"/>
      <property name="username" value="dbo"/>
  </bean>

  <bean id="transactionManagerBean"
    class="org.springframework.jdbc.datasource.
      DataSourceTransactionManager">
```

```
    <constructor-arg ref="dataSourceBean"/>
  </bean>

  <bean id="jdbcTemplateBean"
    class="org.springframework.jdbc.core.JdbcTemplate">
     <property name="dataSource" ref="dataSourceBean"/>
    </bean>
  </beans>
```

We defined a dataSourceBean bean with driverClassName, url, and username. The dataSourceBean reference is passed to the jdbcTemplateBean and transactionManagerBean beans.

2. Spring supports automatic transaction rollback after test execution. It helps us to shield the development database from getting corrupted. A transaction manager bean reference is required to set the test runner before test execution. SpringJUnit4ClassRunner handles the integration tests. Add a PhoneBookDerbySpringDaoIntegrationTest JUnit test and the following lines to it:

```
@ContextConfiguration({ "classpath:integration.xml" })
@TransactionConfiguration(transactionManager =
"transactionManagerBean", defaultRollback = true)
@Transactional
@RunWith(SpringJUnit4ClassRunner.class)
public class PhoneBookDerbySpringDaoIntegrationTest {

  @Autowired
  JdbcTemplate jdbc;

  PhoneBookDerbySpringDao dao;

  @Before
  public void init() {
    dao = new PhoneBookDerbySpringDao(jdbc);
  }

  @Test
  public void integration() throws Exception {
    PhoneEntry entry = newEntry("12345", "Mark", "Smith");

    //test create
    assertTrue(dao.create(entry));
```

```
        //check retrieval
        List<PhoneEntry> phoneEntries =
            dao.searchByFirstName("Mark");

        //check creation
        assertFalse(phoneEntries.isEmpty());

        //update last name
        entry.setLastName("Boucher");

        //update the entry
        assertTrue(dao.update(entry));

        //retrieve the entry by first name
        phoneEntries = dao.searchByFirstName("Mark");

        //verify Mark Boucher exists
        assertFalse(phoneEntries.isEmpty());
        assertEquals("Boucher",
            phoneEntries.get(0).getLastName());

        //delete Mark Boucher from Phonebook
        dao.delete(entry.getPhoneNumber());

        //retrieve entry with first name Mark
        phoneEntries = dao.searchByFirstName("Mark");

        //verify that Mark was deleted
        assertTrue(phoneEntries.isEmpty());
    }
```

The @ContextConfiguration({ "classpath:integration.xml" })
annotation instructs the JUnit runner to load Spring beans from a classpath
location. It will load three beans from the integration.xml file.

The class-level @Transactional annotation makes all methods transactional.

The @TransactionConfiguration(transactionManager =
"transactionManagerBean", defaultRollback = true) annotation
defines the transaction manager, and the defaultRollback attribute tells the
transaction manager to roll back all transactions at the end of a given test.

The following things occur in sequence when the JUnit test is run:

- ° Spring beans are loaded from the `integration.xml` file.
- ° A transaction manager is configured to roll back all transactions.
- ° The `jdbcTemplateBean` bean is wired to the test class member `jdbc`.
- ° The `init` method creates a new instance of the `PhoneBookDerbySpringDao` class and passes `jdbc` to `dao`.
- ° The test gets executed and in turn it creates, updates, and deletes `PhoneEntry`.
- ° After test execution, the transaction manager rolls back the transaction. No data is created, updated, or deleted in the `PhoneBook` table.

3. When the JUnit test is run, the following Spring console log is shown:

```
INFO: Began transaction (1): transaction manager [org.
springframework.jdbc.datasource.DataSourceTransactionManager@56
9c60]; rollback [true]
Apr 11, 2014 10:02:25 PM org.springframework.test.context.
transaction.TransactionalTestExecutionListener endTransaction
INFO: Rolled back transaction after test execution for test
context [[TestContext@134eb84 testClass =
PhoneBookDerbySpringDaoIntegrationTest, testInstance =
com.packt.database.dao.
PhoneBookDerbySpringDaoIntegrationTest@1522de2,
 testMethod =
integration@PhoneBookDerbySpringDaoIntegrationTest,
testException = [null], mergedContextConfiguration =
[MergedContextConfiguration@425743 testClass =
PhoneBookDerbySpringDaoIntegrationTest, locations =
'{classpath:integration.xml}', classes = '{}',
activeProfiles = '{}', contextLoader =
'org.springframework.test.context.support.DelegatingSmartCo
ntextLoader']]]
```

The log shows that a transaction has begun and finally the transaction is rolled back, but the transaction was not rolled back due to any exception, rather it was rolled back due to the [defaultRollback = true] transactional setting. The log shows that `testException = null`, which implies that no exception was thrown.

Summary

This chapter covered every aspect of unit testing the Spring applications. It started with the `TestContext` framework and explored the JUnit 4 enabled `SpringJUnit4ClassRunner`.

We also looked at Spring profiles to work with a different set of configuration files, explored the Spring `Environment` interface, and how to mock the `Environment` interface with `MockEnvironment` and `MockPropertySource`. Moreover, we used the `ReflectionTestUtils` methods to access private fields of the Spring beans, saw the provided usage and examples of Spring annotations for testing, unit tested the MVC application with `MockHttpServletRequest`, `MockHttpSession`, and `ModelAndViewAssert`. We mocked the servlet container with MockMvc to handle actual requests and responses as they will be handled at runtime, and performed real Spring integration and transaction management with the `@Transactional`, `@TransactionConfiguration`, and `@Rollback` annotations.

The next chapter focuses on how to mock Spring beans with Mockito. This chapter covered the integration testing of Spring services, while the next chapter covers the unit testing of the web layer, service layer, and DAO layer with Mockito.

4

Resolving Out-of-container Dependencies with Mockito

The preceding chapter covered the container Spring integration testing and the Spring testing framework. This chapter deals with the role of the Mockito framework in Spring unit testing and how to resolve container dependency with Mockito. The following topics are covered in depth in this chapter:

- Unit testing the service layer with Mockito
- Unit testing the DAO layer with Mockito
- Unit testing the web layer with Mockito

Enterprise applications change over time. There are several reasons for change, such as the addition of new features, bug fixing, improvement in the non functional requirements such as performance or scalability, regulatory changes such as ICD-10 (ICD-10 is the 10th revision of the **International Statistical Classification of Diseases and Related Health Problems (ICD)**, a medical classification list by the **World Health Organization (WHO)**), adapting to modern technology such as implementing JPA, and so on. It doesn't matter how good a software system is, it will be transformed over time. However, a loosely coupled system is more resilient to change than a rigid system. In a tightly coupled system, when we modify a part of the system, the other parts of the system break and we need to fix those parts. This in turn increases the complexity and the degree of reworking required. We should always strive for loose coupling. To minimize coupling, we can divide our system into multiple layers, such as the data access layer, controller layer, service layer, and so on. Once we implement the layers, we can localize the change in one layer without affecting the other layers, such that we can change the data access implementation from Spring JDBC to Hibernate without affecting the service layer.

We'll build a layered Spring web application and unit test each layer. We'll start with the presentation layer and go over to the service and data access layers.

Unit testing the web layer

We'll build a simple Spring web application with the following functionalities:

- User registration
- User login

We'll create the following three layers:

- A data access layer to store and retrieve data
- A service layer to perform business logic and data validation
- Spring controllers to present the UIs and invoke services

In this section, we'll build the controllers and unit test them in isolation from the web server. We have to mock out the service and data access logic.

Perform the following steps to build the web application:

1. Create a dynamic web project, SpringWeb, and copy the Spring JARs from the Spring MVC project we created in *Chapter 1, Getting Familiar with the Spring Framework.*

2. Add the following lines to the web.xml file in order to configure Spring MVC. We have already covered the details in *Chapter 1, Getting Familiar with the Spring Framework*:

```
<web-app xmlns:xsi="...">
  <display-name>SpringWeb</display-name>
  <servlet>
    <servlet-name>dispatcher</servlet-name>
    <servlet-class>
      org.springframework.web.servlet.DispatcherServlet
    </servlet-class>
    <load-on-startup>1</load-on-startup>
  </servlet>
  <servlet-mapping>
    <servlet-name>dispatcher</servlet-name>
    <url-pattern>/</url-pattern>
  </servlet-mapping>
  <context-param>
    <param-name>contextConfigLocation</param-name>
    <param-value>
      /WEB-INF/dispatcher-servlet.xml
    </param-value>
  </context-param>
</web-app>
```

3. Create a `dispatcher-servlet.xml` file under `/WEB-INF` to load the web application context, and add the following line to the file in order to read the bean definitions from a `classpath` application context file called `beans.xml`:

```
<import resource="classpath:beans.xml"/>
```

4. In the source folder, create an XML file called `beans.xml` to define the beans. Add the following lines to the file:

```xml
<?xml version="1.0" encoding="UTF-8"?>
<beans xmlns="http://www.springframework.org/schema/beans"
   xmlns:context="http://www.springframework.org/schema/context"
   xmlns:aop="http://www.springframework.org/schema/aop"
xmlns:tx="http://www.springframework.org/schema/tx"
   xmlns:mvc="http://www.springframework.org/schema/mvc"
xmlns:xsi="http://www.w3.org/2001/XMLSchema-instance"
   xmlns:p="http://www.springframework.org/schema/p"
xmlns:c="http://www.springframework.org/schema/c"
   xsi:schemaLocation="
     http://www.springframework.org/schema/beans
     http://www.springframework.org/schema/beans/spring-beans-
4.1.xsd
     http://www.springframework.org/schema/context
     http://www.springframework.org/schema/context/spring-context-
4.1.xsd
     http://www.springframework.org/schema/tx
     http://www.springframework.org/schema/tx/spring-tx-4.1.xsd
     http://www.springframework.org/schema/aop
     http://www.springframework.org/schema/aop/spring-aop-4.1.xsd
     http://www.springframework.org/schema/mvc
     http://www.springframework.org/schema/mvc/spring-mvc-4.1.xsd">
<mvc:annotation-driven />
<context:component-scan base-package="com.packt" />
<bean
   class="org.springframework.web.servlet.view.
     InternalResourceViewResolver">
<property name="prefix">
  <value>/WEB-INF/pages/</value>
</property>
<property name="suffix">
  <value>.jsp</value>
</property>
</bean>
```

The preceding XML code tells the Spring container to scan the `com.packt` package for bean definitions. MVC is annotation driven and also defines a Spring view resolver bean. The view resolver embodies that a logical view name should be mapped to a physical `.jsp` file under the `/WEB-INF/pages` folder.

5. Create a `login.jsp` page under `/WEB-INF/pages`. Add the following lines to create a login form using the Spring tag library defined in `uri="http://www.springframework.org/tags/form"` and to display a hyperlink for new user sign-up:

```
<%@ taglib prefix="sf" uri="http://www.springframework.org/tags/
form"%>
  <div>
  <h2>Login </h2>
  <sf:form method="POST" action="/SpringWeb/onLogin">
  <fieldset>
    <table cellspacing="0">
      <tr>
        <th><label for="userId">User Id:</label></th>
        <td><input type="text" name="userId"
          id="userId" size="10" maxlength="10"/> </td>
      </tr>
      <tr>
        <th><label for="password">Password:</label></th>
        <td><input type="password" name="password"
          id="password" size="10" maxlength="10"/></td>
      </tr>
      <tr>
        <td colspan="2">
          <input type="submit" value="Submit" /></td>
      </tr>
    </table>
  </fieldset>
  </sf:form>
  </div>
  <h3><a href="/SpringWeb/register">Sign Up</a></h3>
```

Note that the form action is `"/SpringWeb/onLogin"`, which means that when the form is submitted, a Spring controller method annotated with `@RequestMapping({ "/onLogin" })` will handle the processing of the request. The `sf` tag is defined in Spring's `taglib` and `sf:form` represents an HTML form tag.

6. Create a `register.jsp` page under `/WEB-INF/pages` to display user registration. A user can enter the login name, password, first name, and last name, and they also click on the login page hyperlink to go back to the login page. This is how the code for the page will look:

```
<div>
<h2>Register User</h2>
<sf:form method="POST" action="/SpringWeb/onRegistration">
<fieldset>
<table cellspacing="0">
  <tr>
    <th><label for="userId">User Id:</label></th>
    <td><input type="text" name="userId"
      id="userId" size="10" maxlength="10"/></td>
  </tr>
  <tr>
    <th><label for="password">Password:</label></th>
    <td><input type="password" name="password"
      id="password" size="10" maxlength="10"/></td>
  </tr>
  <tr>
    <th><label for="fname">First Name:</label></th>
    <td><input type="fname" name="fname"
      id="fname" size="20" maxlength="20"/></td>
  </tr>
  <tr>
    <th><label for="lname">Last Name:</label></th>
    <td><input type="lname" name="lname"
      id="lname" size="20" maxlength="20"/></td>
  </tr>
  <tr>
    <td colspan="2"><input type="submit"
          value="Submit" /></td>
  </tr>
</table>
</fieldset>
</sf:form>
</div>
<h3><a href="/SpringWeb/login">Login</a></h3>
```

7. We'll create a controller class to display the initial login page and handle the login form submission. Create a `LoginController` class under the `com.packt.controller` package to handle the user login. The `onStartUp` method will return a view named `login` to display the `login.jsp` page, and the method will be annotated with `@RequestMapping({ "/", "/login" })`, which signifies that when a user enters the context path to the browser (the / symbol), the `login.jsp` page is loaded. Also, from the registration page, the user can click on the login (`"/login"`) hyperlink to come back to the login page. The following code snippet shows the `LoginController` class:

```
@Controller
public class LoginController implements Serializable {
private static final long serialVersionUID = 1L;

  @RequestMapping({ "/", "/login" })
  public String onStartUp(ModelMap model) {
    return "login";
  }
}
```

    The `@Controller` annotation signifies that the class is a Spring controller.

8. Create an `onLogin` method to handle the login form submission, and annotate the method with `@RequestMapping({ "/onLogin" })` as we defined the form action on the login page. The method has to validate the username and password against a stored value (the database table). We'll create a request-scoped service to read the user ID and password from the request and then validate the same against the database. We'll call the service `LoginService`. This service will define an `isValid()` method to validate the user credentials. Make the following change to Spring's application context in order to scope the service request and read the user ID and password from the request for validation:

```
<bean id="loginService"
    class="com.packt.controller.LoginService"
    scope="request"
    p:userId="#{request.getParameter('userId')}"
    p:password="#{request.getParameter('password')}">
    <aop:scoped-proxy />
</bean>
```

    We have already covered request-scoped beans, so we will not explain them here again. Make the following changes to the controller class:

```
@RequestMapping({ "/onLogin" })
public ModelAndView onLogin(ModelMap model) {
```

```
if (!loginService.isValid()) {
  model.addAttribute("error", "Invalid user name and
      password");
  return new ModelAndView("login", model);
}

String userName = loginService.retrieveName();
model.addAttribute("name", "Welcome "+userName+"!");
return new ModelAndView("greetings", model);
}
```

If the login fails, it builds an error message that says invalid username or password. Otherwise, `LoginService` retrieves the username for the logged-in user and builds a greeting message.

9. Now, create another controller class to handle the user registration. We'll call this class `RegistrationController`. We need a service to handle user registration, so create a request-scoped service, `RegistrationService`, to read the `userId`, `password`, `firstName`, and `lastName` values, and then validate whether the user ID exists or not. Update the application context to register the request-scoped service, as follows:

```
<bean id="registrationService"
  class="com.packt.controller.RegistrationService"
  scope="request"
  p:userId="#{request.getParameter('userId')}"
  p:password="#{request.getParameter('password')}"
  p:firstName="#{request.getParameter('fname')}"
  p:lastName="#{request.getParameter('lname')}">
  <aop:scoped-proxy />
</bean>
```

Add a `showRegisterView` method and annotate it with `@RequestMapping({ "/register" })` to display the registration page, as shown here:

```
@RequestMapping({ "/register" })
public String showRegisterView(ModelMap model) {
  return "register";
}
```

Add another method, `onRegistration`, to handle the user registration action. We will use the following method:

```
@RequestMapping({ "/onRegistration" })
public ModelAndView onRegistration(ModelMap model) {
  String error = registrationService.hasError();
  if(error != null){
```

```
        model.addAttribute("message", "Cannot create the
            user due to following error ="+error);
    }else{
        model.addAttribute("message", "User created");
    }
     return new ModelAndView("register", model);
}
```

This method delegates the user input validation task to the service; the service returns an error if the user ID exists and then the controller shows the error message to the user, otherwise the user is created.

10. We have created the controller classes, and now we can unit test the controller methods. We'll mock out the services using Mockito. Create a source package, test, for holding the test files and create a com.packt. controller package under test. Add a JUnit test, LoginControllerTest, under com.packt.controller. We need to unit test an invalid login and a successful login scenario. We'll add two tests, as follows:

```
import static org.mockito.Mockito.when;
import static org.junit.Assert.*;
import org.junit.Before;
import org.junit.Test;
import org.junit.runner.RunWith;
import org.mockito.Mock;
import org.mockito.runners.MockitoJUnitRunner;
import org.springframework.ui.ModelMap;
import org.springframework.web.servlet.ModelAndView;


@RunWith(MockitoJUnitRunner.class)
public class LoginControllerTest {
    @Mock
    private LoginService loginService;
    private LoginController controller;

    @Before
    public void setup(){
        controller = new LoginController();
        controller.setLoginService(loginService);
    }

    @Test
    public void when_invalid_login_error_message_is
            _generated() {
```

```
    when(loginService.isValid()).thenReturn(false);
    ModelMap model = new ModelMap();
    ModelAndView modelAndView = controller.onLogin(model);
    assertNotNull(modelAndView.getModel().get("error"));
    assertEquals("login", modelAndView.getViewName());
}

@Test
public void when_a_valid_login_greeting_message_
        is_generated() {
    when(loginService.isValid()).thenReturn(true);
    ModelMap model = new ModelMap();
    ModelAndView modelAndView = controller.onLogin(model);
    assertNull(modelAndView.getModel().get("error"));
    assertNotNull(modelAndView.getModel().get("name"));
    assertEquals("greetings", modelAndView.getViewName());
}

}
```

We created a mock `LoginService` and injected the mocked service to the controller in the setup method. In the case of an invalid login test, we stubbed the `isValid` method to return `false` and then asserted the error and view name. Similarly, in the case of the successful login test, we stubbed the `isValid` method to return `true` and subsequently asserted that no error message was set, and the `greetings` view was returned by the controller.

11. Create a test for `RegistrationController` and mock `RegistrationService`. The following code snippet is the test:

```
@RunWith(MockitoJUnitRunner.class)
public class RegistrationControllerTest {
    @Mock
    private RegistrationService registrationService;
    private RegistrationController controller;

    @Before
    public void setup(){
        controller = new RegistrationController();
        controller.setRegistrationService
            (registrationService);
    }
    @Test
    public void when_invalid_user_id_geneartes_error_message() {
```

```
      when(registrationService.hasError())
        .thenReturn("error");
      ModelMap model = new ModelMap();
      ModelAndView modelAndView = controller.onRegistration(model);
      String message = (String)
          modelAndView.getModel().get("message");
      assertNotNull(message);
      assertTrue
        (message.contains(RegistrationController.ERROR));
    }

    @Test
    public void when_valid_user_id_creates_user() throws Exception {
      when(registrationService.hasError()).thenReturn(null);
      ModelMap model = new ModelMap();
      ModelAndView modelAndView = controller.onRegistration(model);
      String message = (String)
          modelAndView.getModel().get("message");
      assertNotNull(message);
      assertTrue
        (message.contains(RegistrationController.SUCCESS));
    }
  }
```

We unit tested the Spring controllers in isolation from the container. We didn't test the infrastructure, such as Spring annotations. In the next section, we'll unit test the services.

Unit testing the service layer

RegistrationService validates the following rules:

- The user ID, password, first name, or last name cannot be empty
- The first and last names cannot contain numbers
- The first and last names cannot contain special characters
- The password should contain at least one special character
- There cannot be a duplicate user ID

`RegistrationService` should call the database to determine whether a user ID exists or not. We'll create a data access interface for persisting user and to check whether a duplicate user ID is present. Perform the following steps to build the service, create a data access object API, and unit test the service:

1. Create a `RegistrationDao` interface in the `com.packt.dao` package, and add the following methods to check for duplicate users and to create a new user:

```
public interface RegistrationDao {
    boolean isExistingUserId(String userId);
    void create(String userId, String password, String
        firstName, String lastName);
}
```

2. Modify the `RegistrationService` class to have a reference to `RegistrationDao` and its getters/setters, and add the validation logic. The following is the modified method:

```
public String hasError() {
    if (isEmpty(userId)) {
        return "Please enter user id";
    }

    if (isEmpty(password)) {
        return "Please enter password";
    }

    if (isEmpty(firstName)) {
        return "Please enter first name";
    }

    if (isEmpty(lastName)) {
        return "Please enter last name";
    }

    if (isSpecial(firstName) || isSpecial(lastName)) {
        return "Name cannot contain special characters";
    }

    if (isNumeric(firstName) || isNumeric(lastName)) {
        return "Name cannot contain numbers";
    }

    if (!isSpecial(password)) {
```

```
        return "Password should contain a special
            character";
    }

    if (registrationDao.isExistingUserId(userId)) {
        return "User Id exists";
    }
    try {
        registrationDao.create(userId, password,
                firstName, lastName);
    } catch (Exception e) {
        return "Could not create user.";
    }
    return null;
}
```

The class defines three methods for checking special characters, empty Strings, and numeric Strings and then uses these methods for validation. This class calls the `registrationDao.isExistingUserId()` method to check the duplicate user ID and finally calls the `registrationDao.create()` method to create a new user.

3. Now, create a JUnit test, `RegistrationServiceTest`, under the `test` source folder and add the following lines:

```
@RunWith(MockitoJUnitRunner.class)
public class RegistrationServiceTest {
    private RegistrationService registrationService;
    @Mock
    private RegistrationDao registrationDao;
```

Set up the service to use the mock DAO:

```
@Before public void setup(){
    registrationService = new RegistrationService();
    registrationService.setRegistrationDao(registrationDao);
}
```

4. Verify that when any input is empty, the error is shown to the user. It will be sophisticated and handy if we can create small tests for each mandatory field, but I'm creating a big input validation method to reduce code duplication:

```
@Test
public void when_empty_imputs_raises_error() {
    String error = registrationService.hasError();
    assertNotNull(error);
    assertEquals(PLEASE_ENTER_USER_ID, error);
```

```
registrationService.setUserId("john123");
error = registrationService.hasError();
assertNotNull(error);
assertEquals(PLEASE_ENTER_PASSWORD, error);

registrationService.setPassword("Passw@rd");
error = registrationService.hasError();
assertNotNull(error);
assertEquals(PLEASE_ENTER_FIRST_NAME, error);

registrationService.setFirstName("john");
error = registrationService.hasError();
assertNotNull(error);
assertEquals(PLEASE_ENTER_LAST_NAME, error);

registrationService.setLastName("doe");
error = registrationService.hasError();
assertNull(error);
}
```

5. Verify that when the name contains a number, an error is raised:

```
@Test
public void when_name_contains_number_raises_error() {
    registrationService.setFirstName("john1");
    registrationService.setLastName("doe");
    registrationService.setUserId("john123");
    registrationService.setPassword("Passw@rd");
    String error = registrationService.hasError();
    assertNotNull(error);
    assertEquals(NAME_CONTAINS_NUMBER, error);

}
```

6. Verify that when the name contains a special character, such as @, an error is raised:

```
@Test
public void when_name_contains_special
        _chars_raises_error(){
    registrationService.setFirstName("john@");
    registrationService.setLastName("doe");
    registrationService.setUserId("john123");
    registrationService.setPassword("Passw@rd");
```

```
    String error = registrationService.hasError();
    assertNotNull(error);
    assertEquals(NAME_CONTAINS_SPECIAL_CHAR, error);
}
```

7. Stub the DAO's `isExistingUserId()` method using the Mockito API to return `true` in order to emulate a duplicate user ID, and then verify that an error is raised for the duplicate user ID:

```
@Test
public void when_user_exists_raises_error(){
    when(registrationDao.isExistingUserId
        (Mockito.anyString())).thenReturn(true);
    registrationService.setFirstName("john");
    registrationService.setLastName("doe");
    registrationService.setUserId("john123");
    registrationService.setPassword("Passw@rd");
    String error = registrationService.hasError();
    assertNotNull(error);
    assertEquals(USER_ID_EXISTS, error);
}
```

8. Here, stub the void `create()` method to throw an exception using the Mockito API. To emulate this, when a database save fails, no error is percolated and an error message is shown to the user instead:

```
@Test
public void when_user_creation_fails_then_raises_error() {
    doThrow(new RuntimeException("save failed")).
    when(registrationDao).create(anyString(), anyString(),
        anyString(), anyString());
    registrationService.setFirstName("john");
    registrationService.setLastName("doe");
    registrationService.setUserId("john123");
    registrationService.setPassword("Passw@rd");
    String error = registrationService.hasError();
    assertNotNull(error);
    assertEquals(COULD_NOT_CREATE_USER, error);
}
```

9. Finally, check the happy path where the user inputs are valid, user ID is unique, and database save succeeds:

```
@Test
public void when_no_validation_error_then_creates_user(){
    registrationService.setFirstName("john");
    registrationService.setLastName("doe");
```

```
        registrationService.setUserId("john123");
        registrationService.setPassword("Passw@rd");
        assertNull(registrationService.hasError());
    }
}
```

We mocked the database layer and covered the unit testing of the service layer. You can follow the approach and create a JUnit test for the `LoginService`; what you need to do is create an interface for the DAO layer and mock the interface. Next, we'll cover how to mock the database APIs and perform the unit testing of the DAO layer.

Unit testing the data access layer

The data access layer is responsible for managing the database connection, retrieving data from the database, and storing data back to the database. Unit testing the data access layer is very important; if anything goes wrong in this layer, the application will fail. We can unit test the data access logic in isolation from the database and perform integration testing to verify the application and database integrity.

We'll use the Derby database to store real user data. We'll create a utility class to create a database, `derbyDB`, and create a table with details such as `user_data(userId varchar(50)`, `password varchar(50)`, `fname varchar(40)`, and `lname varchar(40))`. Skipping the class details for brevity, you can download the class from the Packt Publishing site. The class name is `DatabaseManager` and the package is `com.packt.dao` under the `src` source package.

The following are the steps to build the Spring DAO layer:

1. Modify the `beans.xml` file to define a data-source and a JDBC template:

```xml
<bean id="dataSource" class="org.springframework.
        jdbc.datasource.DriverManagerDataSource">
  <property name="driverClassName"
      value="org.apache.derby.jdbc.EmbeddedDriver"/>
  <property name="url"
      value="jdbc:derby:derbyDB;create=true"/>
  <property name="username" value="dbo"/>
</bean>

<bean id="transactionManager"
        class="org.springframework.jdbc
        .datasource.DataSourceTransactionManager">
  <constructor-arg ref="dataSource"/>
</bean>
```

```
<bean id="jdbcTemplate" class="org.springframework.
    jdbc.core.JdbcTemplate">
  <property name="dataSource" ref="dataSource"/>
</bean>
```

2. Create a `RegistrationDaoSpring` class and implement `RegistratioDao`. The following is the Spring-enabled DAO class:

```
public class RegistrationDaoSpring implements RegistrationDao {
  private final JdbcTemplate jdbcTemplate;

  public RegistrationDaoSpring(JdbcTemplate jdbcTemplate) {
    this.jdbcTemplate = jdbcTemplate;
  }

@Override
  public boolean isExistingUserId(String userId) {
    return jdbcTemplate.queryForInt(
    "SELECT count(*) FROM user_data where userId=?",
        new Object[] { userId }) > 0;
  }

@Override
  public void create(String userId, String password,
    String firstName, String lastName) {
    int rowCount = jdbcTemplate.update(
      "insert into user_data values
        (?,?,?,?)", new Object[] {
      userId, password, firstName, lastName });
    if (rowCount != 1) {
      throw new RuntimeException("Database update
        row count should be 1");
    }
  }
}
}
```

`JdbcTemplate` simplifies the use of JDBC, as it handles the resources and helps to avoid common errors, such as not closing the connection. It creates and populates the statement object and iterates through `ResultSet`, leaving the application code to provide SQL and extract results.

3. Create a JUnit test class, RegistrationDaoSpringTest, in the com.packt. dao package with the following details:

```
@RunWith(MockitoJUnitRunner.class)
public class RegistrationDaoSpringTest {

  @Mock JdbcTemplate mockJdbcTemplate;
  RegistrationDaoSpring springDao;

  @Before public void init() {
    springDao = new RegistrationDaoSpring(mockJdbcTemplate);
  }
  @Test public void when_creates_user() throws Exception {
    // Prepare data for user registration
    String joesUserId = "joe4u";
    String joesPassword = "joe@123";
    String joesFirstName = "Joseph";
    String joesLastName = "Lawrence";

    // Stub jdbcTemplate's update to return 1
    when(
    mockJdbcTemplate.update(anyString(),
      anyString(), anyObject(), anyObject(),
        anyObject())).thenReturn(1);

    // Execute
    springDao.create(joesUserId, joesPassword,
      joesFirstName, joesLastName);

    // Create argument captures
    ArgumentCaptor<Object> varArgs =
      ArgumentCaptor.forClass(Object.class);

    ArgumentCaptor<String> strArg =
      ArgumentCaptor.forClass(String.class);

    // Verify update method was called and capture args
     verify(mockJdbcTemplate).update(strArg.capture(),
       varArgs.capture(),varArgs.capture(),
       varArgs.capture(), varArgs.capture());

    // Verify 1st dynamic argument was the userId
    assertEquals(joesUserId,
      varArgs.getAllValues().get(0));
    // Verify the password arguments
```

```
    assertEquals(joesPassword,
      varArgs.getAllValues().get(1));
    // Verify the name arguments
    assertEquals(joesFirstName,
      varArgs.getAllValues().get(2));
    assertEquals(joesLastName,
      varArgs.getAllValues().get(3));
  }
```

This JUnit test checks whether the Spring JDBC API is properly used or not and whether the arguments are passed to the JDBC API in the correct order or not. The `ArgumentCaptor` class is a Mockito class and it allows you to capture the argument passed to a stubbed method of a mock/proxy object. Our code calls the `update` method on `jdbcTemplate`. The `update` method takes a SQL String and variable arguments of objects. Now, our task is to verify that the arguments are passed in the proper order, that is, the name is not passed for the password and so on. We use an argument captor to verify the argument order:

```
@Test(expected=RuntimeException.class)
public void when_create_fails_then_raises_error(){
    // Prepare data for user registration
    String joesUserId = "joe4u";
    String joesPassword = "joe@123";
    String joesFirstName = "Joseph";
    String joesLastName = "Lawrence";

    // Stub jdbcTemplate's update  to return no update
    when(mockJdbcTemplate.update(anyString(),
      anyString(), anyObject(),anyObject(),
      anyObject())).thenReturn(0);

    // Execute for fail
    springDao.create(joesUserId, joesPassword,
      joesFirstName, joesLastName);
  }

}
```

4. We have unit tested the DAO layer in isolation from database. Now, we need to verify the integrity of our application. We'll do end-to-end testing. Modify the `beans.xml` file to define `registrationDaoSpring`, as follows:

```
<bean id="registrationDaoSpring"
    class="com.packt.dao.RegistrationDaoSpring">
  <constructor-arg ref="jdbcTemplate" />
</bean>
```

5. Autowire the DAO to the `RegisterService` as follows:

```
@Autowired
private RegistrationDao registrationDao;
```

6. Now, run the application and click on the **Sign Up** hyperlink to load the registration page. In the registration page, enter the user ID, password, first and last names, and then click on the **Submit** button:

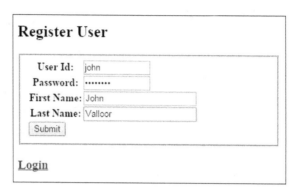

7. The system will create the user and display the following screen:

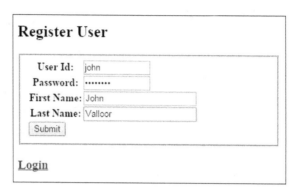

8. When we try to create a duplicate user, the following message is displayed:

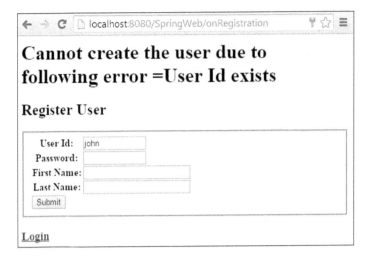

We created a layered architecture and learned how to unit test individual layers in isolation from other layers, and then we finally integrated the application. Integration becomes easier when each individual layer is unit tested.

Summary

This chapter covered unit testing of the service layer in isolation from the data access layer with Mockito, unit testing the Spring data access layer with Mockito, and unit testing the Spring presentation layer (MVC) with Mockito.

The next chapter explores the new features of Spring 4 and its advanced topics, such as @RestController, AsyncRestTemplate, Async task, and caching.

5
Time Travelling with Spring

Spring 4.0 is the Java 8-enabled latest release of the Spring Framework. In this chapter, we'll discover the major changes in the Spring 4.x release and the four important features of the Spring 4 framework. We will cover the following topics in depth:

- `@RestController`
- `AsyncRestTemplate`
- Async tasks
- Caching

Discovering the new Spring release

This section deals with the new features and enhancements in Spring Framework 4.0. The following are the features:

- Spring 4 supports Java 8 features such as Java lambda expressions and `java.time`. Spring 4 supports JDK 6 as the minimum.
- All deprecated packages/methods are removed.
- Java Enterprise Edition 6 or 7 are the base of Spring 4, which is based on JPA 2 and Servlet 3.0.
- Bean configuration using the Groovy DSL is supported in Spring Framework 4.0.
- Hibernate 4.3 is supported by Spring 4.
- Custom annotations are supported in Spring 4.
- Autowired lists and arrays can be ordered. The `@Order` annotation and the `Ordered` interface are supported.

- The @Lazy annotation can now be used on injection points as well as on the @Bean definitions.

- For the REST application, Spring 4 provides a new @RestController annotation. We will discuss this in detail in the following section.

- The AsyncRestTemplate feature (class) is added for asynchronous REST client development.

- Different time zones are supported in Spring 4.0.

- New spring-websocket and spring-messaging modules have been added.

- The SocketUtils class is added to examine the free TCP and UDP server ports on localhost.

- All the mocks under the org.springframework.mock.web package are now based on the Servlet 3.0 specification.

- Spring supports JCache annotations and new improvements have been made in caching.

- The @Conditional annotation has been added to conditionally enable or disable an @Configuration class or even individual @Bean methods.

- In the test module, SQL script execution can now be configured declaratively via the new @Sql and @SqlConfig annotations on a per-class or per-method basis.

You can visit the Spring Framework reference at http://docs.spring.io/spring/docs/4.1.2.BUILD-SNAPSHOT/spring-framework-reference/htmlsingle/#spring-whats-new for more details.

Also, you can watch a video at http://zeroturnaround.com/rebellabs/spring-4-on-java-8-geekout-2013-video/ for more details on the changes in Spring 4.

Working with asynchronous tasks

Java 7 has a feature called Future. Futures let you retrieve the result of an asynchronous operation at a later time. The FutureTask class runs in a separate thread, which allows you to perform non-blocking asynchronous operations. Spring provides an @Async annotation to make it more easier to use. We'll explore Java's Future feature and Spring's @Async declarative approach:

1. Create a project, TimeTravellingWithSpring, and add a package, com.packt.async.

2. We'll exercise a bank's use case, where an automated job will run and settle loan accounts. It will also find all the defaulters who haven't paid the loan EMI for a month and then send an SMS to their number. The job takes time to process thousands of accounts, so it will be good if we can send SMSes asynchronously to minimize the burden of the job. We'll create a service class to represent the job, as shown in the following code snippet:

```
@Service
public class AccountJob {
    @Autowired
    private SMSTask smsTask;

    public void process() throws InterruptedException,
            ExecutionException {
    System.out.println("Going to find defaulters... ");

    Future<Boolean> asyncResult =smsTask.send("1", "2", "3");
    System.out.println("Defaulter Job Complete. SMS will be
            sent to all defaulter");

    Boolean result = asyncResult.get();
    System.out.println("Was SMS sent? " + result);
    }
}
```

The job class autowires an SMSTask class and invokes the send method with phone numbers. The send method is executed asynchronously and Future is returned. When the job calls the get() method on Future, a result is returned. If the result is not processed before the get() method invocation, the ExecutionException is thrown. We can use a timeout version of the get() method.

3. Create the SMSTask class in the com.packt.async package with the following details:

```
@Component
public class SMSTask {

    @Async
    public Future<Boolean>  send(String... numbers) {
    System.out.println("Selecting SMS format   ");

    try {
      Thread.sleep(2000);
    } catch (InterruptedException e) {
```

```
      e.printStackTrace();
      return new AsyncResult<>(false);
  }
  System.out.println("Async SMS send task is Complete!!!");
  return new AsyncResult<>(true);
  }
}
```

Note that the method returns `Future`, and the method is annotated with `@Async` to signify asynchronous processing.

4. Create a JUnit test to verify asynchronous processing:

```
@RunWith(SpringJUnit4ClassRunner.class)
@ContextConfiguration(locations="classpath:com/packt/async/
        applicationContext.xml")
public class AsyncTaskExecutionTest {

  @Autowired ApplicationContext context;

  @Test
  public void jobTest() throws Exception {
    AccountJob job =
          (AccountJob) context.getBean(AccountJob.class);
    job.process();
  }
}
```

The `job` bean is retrieved from the `applicationContext` file and then the `process` method is called. When we execute the test, the following output is displayed:

```
Going to find defaulters...
Defaulter Job Complete. SMS will be sent to all defaulter
Selecting SMS format
Async SMS send task is Complete!!!
Was SMS sent? true
```

During execution, you might feel that the async task is executed after a delay of 2 seconds as the `SMSTask` class waits for 2 seconds.

Exploring @RestController

JAX-RS provides the functionality for **Representational State Transfer (RESTful)** web services. REST is well-suited for basic, ad hoc integration scenarios. Spring MVC offers controllers to create RESTful web services.

In Spring MVC 3.0, we need to explicitly annotate a class with the `@Controller` annotation in order to specify a controller servlet and annotate each and every method with `@ResponseBody` to serve JSON, XML, or a custom media type. With the advent of the Spring 4.0 `@RestController` stereotype annotation, we can combine `@ResponseBody` and `@Controller`.

The following example will demonstrate the usage of `@RestController`:

1. Create a dynamic web project, `RESTfulWeb`.

2. Modify the `web.xml` file and add a configuration to intercept requests with a Spring `DispatcherServlet`:

```
<web-app xmlns:xsi="http://www.w3.org/2001/XMLSchema-instance"
xmlns="http://java.sun.com/xml/ns/javaee" xmlns:web="http://java.
sun.com/xml/ns/javaee/web-app_2_5.xsd" xsi:schemaLocation="http://
java.sun.com/xml/ns/javaee http://java.sun.com/xml/ns/javaee/web-
app_3_0.xsd" id="WebApp_ID" version="3.0">
  <display-name>RESTfulWeb</display-name>
  <servlet>
    <servlet-name>dispatcher</servlet-name>
    <servlet-class>
          org.springframework.web.servlet.DispatcherServlet
    </servlet-class>
    <load-on-startup>1</load-on-startup>
  </servlet>
  <servlet-mapping>
    <servlet-name>dispatcher</servlet-name>
    <url-pattern>/</url-pattern>
  </servlet-mapping>
  <context-param>
    <param-name>contextConfigLocation</param-name>
    <param-value>
      /WEB-INF/dispatcher-servlet.xml
    </param-value>
  </context-param>
</web-app>
```

3. The `DispatcherServlet` expects a configuration file with the naming convention `[servlet-name]-servlet.xml`. Create an application context XML, `dispatcher-servlet.xml`. We'll use annotations to configure Spring beans, so we need to tell the Spring container to scan the Java package in order to craft the beans. Add the following lines to the application context in order to instruct the container to scan the `com.packt.controller` package:

```
<context:component-scan base-package=
  "com.packt.controller" />
<mvc:annotation-driven />
```

4. We need a REST controller class to handle the requests and generate a JSON output. Go to the `com.packt.controller` package and add a `SpringService` controller class. To configure the class as a REST controller, we need to annotate it with the `@RestController` annotation. The following code snippet represents the class:

```
@RestController
@RequestMapping("/hello")
public class SpringService {
   private Set<String> names = new HashSet<String>();
   @RequestMapping(value = "/{name}", method =
         RequestMethod.GET)
   public String displayMsg(@PathVariable String name) {
     String result = "Welcome " + name;
     names.add(name);
     return result;
   }

   @RequestMapping(value = "/all/", method =
         RequestMethod.GET)
   public String anotherMsg() {

     StringBuilder result = new StringBuilder("We
         greeted so far ");
     for(String name:names){
       result.append(name).append(", ");
     }
     return result.toString();
   }
}
```

We annotated the class with `@RequestMapping("/hello")`. This means that the `SpringService` class will cater for the requests with the `http://{site}/{context}/hello` URL pattern, or since we are running the app in localhost, the URL can be `http://localhost:8080/RESTfulWeb/hello`.

The `displayMsg` method is annotated with `@RequestMapping(value = "/{name}", method = RequestMethod.GET)`. So, the method will handle all HTTP GET requests with the URL pattern `/hello/{name}`. The name can be any String, such as `/hello/xyz` or `/hello/john`. In turn, the method stores the name to `Set` for later use and returns a greeting message, `welcome {name}`.

The `anotherMsg` method is annotated with `@RequestMapping(value = "/all/", method = RequestMethod.GET)`, which means that the method accepts all the requests with the `http://{SITE}/{Context}/hello/all/` URL pattern. Moreover, this method builds a list of all users who visited the `/hello/{names}` URL. Remember, the `displayMsg` method stores the names in `Set`; this method iterates `Set` and builds a list of names who visited the `/hello/{name}` URL.

There is some confusion though: what will happen if you enter the `/hello/all` URL in the browser? When we pass only a String literal after `/hello/`, the `displayMsg` method handles it, so you will be greeted with `welcome all`. However, if you type `/hello/all/` instead — note that we added a slash after `all` — it means that the URL does not match the `/hello/{name}` pattern and the second method will handle the request and show you the list of users who visited the first URL.

5. When we run the application and access the `/hello/{name}` URL, the following output is displayed:

When we access `http://localhost:8080/RESTfulWeb/hello/all/`, the following output is displayed:

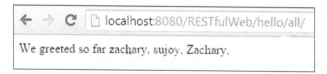

Therefore, our RESTful application is ready for use, but just remember that in the real world, you need to secure the URLs against unauthorized access. In a web service, development security plays a key role. You can read the Spring security reference manual for additional information.

Learning AsyncRestTemplate

We live in a small, wonderful world where everybody is interconnected and impatient! We are interconnected through technology and applications, such as social networks, Internet banking, telephones, chats, and so on. Likewise, our applications are interconnected; often, an application housed in India may need to query an external service hosted in Philadelphia to get some significant information.

We are impatient as we expect everything to be done in seconds; we get frustrated when we make an HTTP call to a remote service, and this blocks the processing unless the remote response is back. We cannot finish everything in milliseconds or nanoseconds, but we can process long-running tasks asynchronously or in a separate thread, allowing the user to work on something else.

To handle RESTful web service calls asynchronously, Spring offers two useful classes: `AsyncRestTemplate` and `ListenableFuture`. We can make an async call using the template and get `Future` back and then continue with other processing, and finally we can ask `Future` to get the result.

This section builds an asynchronous RESTful client to query the RESTful web service we developed in the preceding section. The `AsyncRestTemplate` class defines an array of overloaded methods to access RESTful web services asynchronously. We'll explore the `exchange` and `execute` methods.

The following are the steps to explore the template:

1. Create a package, `com.packt.rest.template`.

2. Add a `AsyncRestTemplateTest` JUnit test.

3. Create an `exchange()` test method and add the following lines:

```
@Test
  public void exchange(){
    AsyncRestTemplate asyncRestTemplate = new
      AsyncRestTemplate();
    String url ="http://localhost:8080/RESTfulWeb/
      hello/all/";
    HttpMethod method = HttpMethod.GET;
    Class<String> responseType = String.class;

    HttpHeaders headers = new HttpHeaders();
    headers.setContentType(MediaType.TEXT_PLAIN);

    HttpEntity<String> requestEntity = new
      HttpEntity<String>("params", headers);
```

```
ListenableFuture<ResponseEntity<String>> future =
  asyncRestTemplate.exchange(url, method,
  requestEntity, responseType);
try {
  //waits for the result
  ResponseEntity<String> entity = future.get();
  //prints body of the given URL
  System.out.println(entity.getBody());
} catch (InterruptedException e) {
  e.printStackTrace();
} catch (ExecutionException e) {
  e.printStackTrace();
}
}
```

The exchange() method has six overloaded versions. We used the method that takes a URL, an HttpMethod method such as GET or POST, an HttpEntity method to set the header, and finally a response type class. We called the exchange method, which in turn called the execute method and returned ListenableFuture. The ListenableFuture is the handle to our output; we invoked the GET method on ListenableFuture to get the RESTful service call response. The ResponseEntity has the getBody, getClass, getHeaders, and getStatusCode methods for extracting the web service call response.

We invoked the http://localhost:8080/RESTfulWeb/hello/all/ URL and got back the following response:

```
Console ⊠
<terminated> AsyncRestTemplateTest (1) [JUnit] C:\Program Files\Java\jre7\
log4j:WARN No appenders could be found for logger
log4j:WARN Please initialize the log4j system properly.
We greeted so far zachary, sujoy, Zachary,
```

4. Now, create an execute test method and add the following lines:

```
@Test public void execute(){
  AsyncRestTemplate asyncTemp = new AsyncRestTemplate();
  String url ="http://localhost:8080/RESTfulWeb
    /hello/reader";
  HttpMethod method = HttpMethod.GET;

  HttpHeaders headers = new HttpHeaders();
  headers.setContentType(MediaType.TEXT_PLAIN);
```

```
AsyncRequestCallback requestCallback = new
  AsyncRequestCallback (){
  @Override
  public void doWithRequest (AsyncClientHttpRequest
    request)  throws IOException {
    System.out.println (request.getURI ());
  }
};
ResponseExtractor<String> responseExtractor = new
  ResponseExtractor<String>(){
  @Override
    public String extractData (ClientHttpResponse
      response) throws IOException {
      return response.getStatusText ();
  }
};

Map<String,String> urlVariable = new HashMap<String,
  String>();
ListenableFuture<String> future = asyncTemp.execute(url,
  method, requestCallback, responseExtractor,
  urlVariable);
  try {
    //wait for the result
    String result = future.get ();
    System.out.println("Status =" +result);
  } catch (InterruptedException e) {
    e.printStackTrace();
  } catch (ExecutionException e) {
    e.printStackTrace();
  }
}
```

The execute method has several variants. We invoke the one that takes a
URL, HttpMethod such as GET or POST, an AsyncRequestCallback method
which is invoked from the execute method just before executing the request
asynchronously, a ResponseExtractor to extract the response, such as a
response body, status code or headers, and a URL variable such as a URL
that takes parameters. We invoked the execute method and received a
future, as our ResponseExtractor extracts the status code. So, when we ask
the future to get the result, it returns the response status which is OK or 200.
In the AsyncRequestCallback method, we invoked the request URI; hence,
the output first displays the request URI and then prints the response status.

The following is the output:

```
<terminated> AsyncRestTemplateTest (1) [JUnit] C:\Program Files\Java\jre7\bin\javaw.exe

calling
http://localhost:8080/RESTfulWeb/hello/reader
log4j:WARN No appenders could be found for logger
log4j:WARN Please initialize the log4j system properly.
Status =OK
```

Caching objects

Scalability is a major concern in web application development. Generally, most web traffic is focused on some special set of information. So, only those records are queried very often. If we can cache these records, then the performance and scalability of the system will increase immensely.

The Spring Framework provides support for adding caching into an existing Spring application. In this section, we'll work with EhCache, the most widely used caching solution. Download the latest EhCache JAR from the Maven repository; the URL to download version 2.7.2 is `http://mvnrepository.com/artifact/net.sf.ehcache/ehcache/2.7.2`.

Spring provides two annotations for caching: `@Cacheable` and `@CacheEvict`. These annotations allow methods to trigger cache population or cache eviction, respectively.

The `@Cacheable` annotation is used to identify a cacheable method, which means that for an annotate method the result is stored into the cache. Therefore, on subsequent invocations (with the same arguments), the value in the cache is returned without actually executing the method.

The cache abstraction allows the eviction of cache for removing stale or unused data from the cache. The `@CacheEvict` annotation demarcates the methods that perform cache eviction, that is, methods that act as triggers to remove data from the cache.

The following are the steps to build a cacheable application with EhCache:

1. Create a serializable `Employee` POJO class in the `com.packt.cache` package to store the employee ID and name. The following is the class definition:

```java
public class Employee implements Serializable {
  private static final long serialVersionUID = 1L;
  private final String firstName, lastName, empId;

  public Employee(String empId, String fName, String lName) {
    this.firstName = fName;
```

```
      this.lastName = lName;
      this.empId = empId;
   }
   //Getter methods
}
```

2. Spring caching supports two storages: the `ConcurrentMap` and `ehcache` libraries. To configure caching, we need to configure a manager in the application context. The `org.springframework.cache.ehcache.EhCacheCacheManager` class manages ehcache. Then, we need to define a cache with a `configurationLocation` attribute. The `configurationLocation` attribute defines the configuration resource. The ehcache-specific configuration is read from the resource `ehcache.xml`.

   Create an `applicationConext` file under the `com.packt.cache` package with the following details:

```xml
<beans xmlns="http://www.springframework.org/schema/beans"
xmlns:xsi="http://www.w3.org/2001/XMLSchema-instance"
xmlns:context="http://www.springframework.org/schema/context"
xmlns:cache="http://www.springframework.org/schema/cache"
xmlns:p="http://www.springframework.org/schema/p"
xsi:schemaLocation="
http://www.springframework.org/schema/beans
http://www.springframework.org/schema/beans/spring-beans-
4.1.xsd
http://www.springframework.org/schema/cache http://www.
springframework.org/schema/cache/spring-cache-
4.1.xsd
http://www.springframework.org/schema/context http://www.
springframework.org/schema/context/spring-
context-4.1.xsd ">
    <context:component-scan base-package=
     "com.packt.cache" />
    <cache:annotation-driven/>

    <bean id="cacheManager" class="org.springframework.cache.
          ehcache.EhCacheCacheManager"
      p:cacheManager-ref="ehcache"/>
    <bean id="ehcache" class="org.springframework.cache.
    ehcache.EhCacheManagerFactoryBean"
      p:configLocation="classpath:com/packt/cache/ehcache.xml"/>
</beans>
```

The `<cache:annotation-driven/>` tag informs the Spring container that the caching and eviction is performed in annotated methods. We defined a `cacheManager` bean and then defined an `ehcache` bean. The `ehcache` bean's `configLocation` points to an `ehcache.xml` file. We'll create the file next.

3. Create an XML file, `ehcache.xml`, under the `com.packt.cache` package and add the following cache configuration data:

```
<ehcache>
    <diskStore path="java.io.tmpdir"/>
    <cache name="employee"
           maxElementsInMemory="100"
           eternal="false"
           timeToIdleSeconds="120"
           timeToLiveSeconds="120"
           overflowToDisk="true"
           maxElementsOnDisk="10000000"
           diskPersistent="false"
           diskExpiryThreadIntervalSeconds="120"
           memoryStoreEvictionPolicy="LRU"/>

</ehcache>
```

The XML configures many things. Cache is stored in memory, but memory has a limit, so we need to define `maxElementsInMemory`. EhCache needs to store data to disk when max elements in memory reaches the threshold limit. We provide `diskStore` for this purpose. The eviction policy is set as an LRU, but the most important thing is the cache name. The name `employee` will be used to access the cache configuration.

4. Now, create a service to store the `Employee` objects in a HashMap. The following is the service:

```
@Service
public class EmployeeService {
    private final Map<String, Employee> employees = new
      ConcurrentHashMap<String, Employee>();

    @PostConstruct
    public void init() {
        saveEmployee (new Employee("101", "John", "Doe"));
        saveEmployee (new Employee("102", "Jack",
          "Russell"));
    }
```

```
    @Cacheable("employee")
    public Employee getEmployee(final String employeeId) {
      System.out.println(String.format("Loading a
        employee with id of : %s", employeeId));
      return employees.get(employeeId);
    }

    @CacheEvict(value = "employee", key = "#emp.empId")
    public void saveEmployee(final Employee emp) {
      System.out.println(String.format("Saving a emp with
        id of : %s", emp.getEmpId()));
      employees.put(emp.getEmpId(), emp);
    }
}
```

The getEmployee method is a cacheable method; it uses the cache employee. When the getEmployee method is invoked more than once with the same employee ID, the object is returned from the cache instead of the original method being invoked. The saveEmployee method is a CacheEvict method.

5. Now, we'll examine caching. We'll call the getEmployee method twice; the first call will populate the cache and the subsequent call will be responded to by the cache. Create a JUnit test, CacheConfiguration, and add the following lines:

```
@RunWith(SpringJUnit4ClassRunner.class)
@ContextConfiguration(locations="classpath:com/packt/cache/
applicationContext.xml")
public class CacheConfiguration {
    @Autowired
    ApplicationContext context;

@Test public void jobTest() throws Exception {
  EmployeeService employeeService =
      (EmployeeService)context.getBean(EmployeeService.class);

  long time = System.currentTimeMillis();
  employeeService.getEmployee("101");
  System.out.println("time taken
    ="+(System.currentTimeMillis() - time));

  time = System.currentTimeMillis();
  employeeService.getEmployee("101");
```

```
    System.out.println("time taken to read from cache
      ="+(System.currentTimeMillis() - time));

    time = System.currentTimeMillis();
    employeeService.getEmployee("102");
    System.out.println("time taken
          ="+(System.currentTimeMillis() - time));

    time = System.currentTimeMillis();
    employeeService.getEmployee("102");
    System.out.println("time taken to read from cache
      ="+(System.currentTimeMillis() - time));

    employeeService.saveEmployee(new Employee("1000",
      "Sujoy", "Acharya"));

    time = System.currentTimeMillis();
    employeeService.getEmployee("1000");
    System.out.println("time taken
      ="+(System.currentTimeMillis() - time));

    time = System.currentTimeMillis();
    employeeService.getEmployee("1000");
    System.out.println("time taken to read from cache
      ="+(System.currentTimeMillis() - time));
    }

}
```

Note that the getEmployee method is invoked twice for each employee, and we recorded the method execution time in milliseconds. You will find from the output that every second call is answered by the cache, as the first call prints **Loading a employee with id of : 101** and then the next call doesn't print the message but prints the time taken to execute. You will also find that the time taken for the cached objects is zero or less than the method invocation time.

The following screenshot shows the output:

```
Loading a employee with id of : 101
time taken =31
time taken to read from cache =0
Loading a employee with id of : 102
time taken =1
time taken to read from cache =0
Saving a emp with id of : 1000
Loading a employee with id of : 1000
time taken =1
time taken to read from cache =0
```

Summary

This chapter started with discovering the features of the new major Spring release 4.0, such as Java 8 support and so on. Then, we picked four Spring 4 topics and explored them one by one.

The @Async section showcased the execution of long-running methods asynchronously and provided an example of how to handle asynchronous processing.

The @RestController section eased the RESTful web service development with the advent of the @RestController annotation.

The AsyncRestTemplate section explained the RESTful client code to invoke RESTful web service asynchronously.

Caching is inevitable for a high-performance, scalable web application. The caching section explained the EhCache and Spring integrations to achieve a high-availability caching solution.

Index

Symbols

V

verify
  atLeast(int minNumberOfInvocations) 87
  atLeastOnce() 87
  atMost(int maxNumberOfInvocations) 87
  never() 87
  only() 87
  timeout(int millis) 87
  times(int wantedNumberOfInvocations) 87
video
  URL 144

W

weaving 26
web layer
  about 12
  Portlet 12
  unit testing 124-132
  Webmvc 12
  WebSocket 12
World Health Organization (WHO) 123

Thank you for buying
Mockito for Spring

About Packt Publishing

Packt, pronounced 'packed', published its first book, *Mastering phpMyAdmin for Effective MySQL Management*, in April 2004, and subsequently continued to specialize in publishing highly focused books on specific technologies and solutions.

Our books and publications share the experiences of your fellow IT professionals in adapting and customizing today's systems, applications, and frameworks. Our solution-based books give you the knowledge and power to customize the software and technologies you're using to get the job done. Packt books are more specific and less general than the IT books you have seen in the past. Our unique business model allows us to bring you more focused information, giving you more of what you need to know, and less of what you don't.

Packt is a modern yet unique publishing company that focuses on producing quality, cutting-edge books for communities of developers, administrators, and newbies alike. For more information, please visit our website at www.packtpub.com.

About Packt Open Source

In 2010, Packt launched two new brands, Packt Open Source and Packt Enterprise, in order to continue its focus on specialization. This book is part of the Packt Open Source brand, home to books published on software built around open source licenses, and offering information to anybody from advanced developers to budding web designers. The Open Source brand also runs Packt's Open Source Royalty Scheme, by which Packt gives a royalty to each open source project about whose software a book is sold.

Writing for Packt

We welcome all inquiries from people who are interested in authoring. Book proposals should be sent to author@packtpub.com. If your book idea is still at an early stage and you would like to discuss it first before writing a formal book proposal, then please contact us; one of our commissioning editors will get in touch with you.

We're not just looking for published authors; if you have strong technical skills but no writing experience, our experienced editors can help you develop a writing career, or simply get some additional reward for your expertise.

Mockito Essentials

ISBN: 978-1-78398-360-5   Paperback: 214 pages

A practical guide to get you up and running with unit testing using Mockito

1. Explore Mockito features and learn stubbing, mocking and spying dependencies using the Mockito framework.

2. Mock external dependencies for legacy and greenfield projects and create an automated JUnit safety net for building reliable, maintainable and testable software.

3. A focused guide filled with examples and supporting illustrations on testing your software using Mockito.

Mastering Unit Testing Using Mockito and JUnit

ISBN: 9781-7-8398-250-9   Paperback: 314 pages

An advanced guide to mastering unit testing using Mockito and JUnit

1. Create meaningful and maintainable automated unit tests using advanced JUnit features and the Mockito framework.

2. Build an automated continuous integration environment to get real-time feedback on broken code, code coverage, code quality, and integration issues.

3. Covers best practices and presents insights on architecture and designs to create faster and reliable unit testing environments.

Please check **www.PacktPub.com** for information on our titles

Mockito Cookbook

ISBN: 978-1-78398-274-5   Paperback: 284 pages

Over 65 recipes to get you up and running with unit testing using Mockito

1. Implement best practices to perform tests with Mockito.

2. Extend Mockito with other popular Java-based unit testing frameworks such as JUnit and Powermock.

3. A focused guide with many recipes on testing your software using Mockito.

Test-Driven Development with Mockito

ISBN: 978-1-78328-329-3   Paperback: 172 pages

Learn how to apply Test-Driven Development and the Mockito framework in real life projects, using realistic, hands-on examples

1. Start writing clean, high quality code to apply Design Patterns and principles.

2. Add new features to your project by applying Test-first development- JUnit 4.0 and Mockito framework.

3. Make legacy code testable and clean up technical debts.

Please check **www.PacktPub.com** for information on our titles

www.ingramcontent.com/pod-product-compliance
Lightning Source LLC
LaVergne TN
LVHW081343050326
832903LV00024B/1287